GROWING UP AMONG SAILORS

Growing Up Among Sailors

J. Ifor Davies

First published in 1983 by Gwynedd Archives Service
New digital edition: Gwasg Carreg Gwalch 2020

© David Michael Davies on behalf of J. Ifor Davies Estate

All rights reserved. No part of this publication
may be reproduced, stored in a retrieval system,
or transmitted in any form or by any means, electronic,
electrostatic, magnetic tape, mechanical, photocopying,
recording, or otherwise, without prior permission
of the authors of the works herein.

ISBN: 978-1-84527-705-5

Cover design: Eleri Owen

Published by Gwasg Carreg Gwalch,
12 Iard yr Orsaf, Llanrwst, Wales LL26 0EH
tel: 01492 642031
email: books@carreg-gwalch.cymru
website: www.carreg-gwalch.cymru

Contents

Foreword (Aled Eames)		7
Acknowledgements		9
The Setting		11
1.	Roots	17
2.	1879-1903	24
3.	Gwydyr Castle: Voyage 1	37
4.	Gwydyr Castle: Voyages 2 & 3	63
5.	Gwydyr Castle: Voyage 4	73
6.	Dry Land	78
7.	Finding one's bearings	85
8.	Two Years of Peace	90
9.	The 1914-18 War	96
10.	Aftermath of War	108
11.	The Monkbarns	113
12.	Discovering Nefyn	129
13.	The Perils of Illiteracy	146
14.	Background Activities	155
15.	School and Chapel	162
16.	The Beach	181
17.	The Sea and Seamen	189
18.	Disaster and Bad News	201
19.	Two Short Voyages	206
20.	Bruges and Birkenhead	214
21.	A Hurricane	225
22.	Homeward Bound	234
23.	A Tradition Ends	246
Epilogue		250
A review by Iorwerth Roberts of the first edition of Growing Up Among Sailors, Daily Post, 1983		252

To the memory of
MY PARENTS
and to
MY WIFE AND FAMILY

Our late father's book, originally published in 1983, has proved to be an invaluable source of information for local and maritime historians, both in Wales and further afield. Unfortunately, it has been out of print for some time.

Since its publication, new information has come to our attention. In this revised edition we have taken the opportunity to include some of these, and also to correct some minor innaccuracies, either typographical or factual.

We wish to acknowledge with thanks the help and co-operation received from Gwynedd Archives Service.

John & David Davies
January 2020

Foreword

Ifor Davies in this exceptionally well written book has evocatively recreated not only the life of his own community in Nefyn and aboard the fine full rigged ships which his father commanded with such distinction, but has also recreated experiences which were common to men and women who earned their living at sea in maritime communities from the Åland Islands to San Fransisco, from the coasts of Maine to Newcastle, New South Wales, Ceredigion to Callao.

Some thirty years ago, the late David Thomas, in his admirable pioneering work *Hen Longau Sir Gaernarfon*, drew attention to the remarkable and as yet largely untold story of the maritime communities of North West Wales in the nineteenth and early twentieth centuries. In Wales, curiously enough, novelists and short story writers, as well as historians have found the slate quarries and coal mines of much greater interest than the lives and activities of the men who manned the ships which carried the slate and coal to ports great and small in many parts of the world. In an age when the commercial and political importance of the merchant fleet of Britain was unquestioned, its seamen were drawn largely from remote, non-industrialised areas such as the West of Scotland, South West and North East England, North and West Wales. And there are many similarities between the villages where these seamen grew up and the coastal villages of, say, Scandinavia or North America. Amongst everywhere the way of life which characterised these communities has gone forever; villages where almost every cottage bred a family of seamen now have only a handful of men who earn their living at sea. Nowhere is this change more apparent than in North Wales and, in particular, the Lleyn peninsula.

Much first hand information from seamen and their contemporaries has disappeared within the last two generations and it is almost too late to tap this rich vein of Welsh history. It is therefore all the more fortunate that the Gwynedd Archives Service has persuaded Ifor Davies to write his own account of his youth in the ancient fishing village of Nefyn where he grew up, and those far off early years which he and his sister spent sailing the world with their mother and father. Captain William Davies commanded the *Eivion*, the *Gwydyr Castle*, the *Belford* and the *Monkbarns*, all well known Cape Horn sailing ships. Among those who served under Captain Davies was the late Captain Malcolm Bruce Glasier, a leading figure in the maritime world, some of whose fine photographs of the *Monkbarns* are reproduced in this book; many will remember the high regard Captain Glasier always had for Captain William Davies's qualities as a superb seaman and quite remarkable man.

When the *Monkbarns*, the last full rigged British ship to round Cape Horn with a cargo, came quietly into the Thames after an epic voyage in July 1926, sadly without her master, the age of sail was almost over, but to his young family in Nefyn it must have appeared much more than the end of an age. It is our privilege, however, thanks to Ifor Davies's modest but finely written account to enter that age; Nefyn and its seamen, the wives who sailed with them, and the families who waited for their return, come alive and enable us to recognize the richness of our heritage.

Aled Eames
Maritime Historian
and founder editor of Maritime Wales

Acknowledgements

During the first quarter of this century I enjoyed the privilege of belonging to a community which, over a period of several generations, had established strong and extensive links with the sea and regularly produced more sailors to the square yard than any other part of the British Isles. The Census figures for 1931 show that a local population of fewer than 1,300 included 69 Master Mariners. The pages which follow are an attempt to describe, or at least to suggest, what it was like to grow up against such a background at that particular stage in its history.

For my material I have had to rely mainly upon my own personal recollections, but much of it is based upon information provided by relatives and friends, often in haphazard fashion, or gleaned more by luck than good management from old postcards, letters, or family Bibles. For the early and the later sections I have been heavily indebted to former shipmates of my father – men like Captain Richard Davies of Nefyn, Captain W. H. Hughes of Blyth, Captain M. B. Glasier of West Kirby, and Captain Griff. Roberts of Borthygest – who were in a position to speak at first hand of incidents which occurred before I was born or of which I had no direct personal knowledge. Books, too, have played a vital part. For the description of some events at sea I have drawn freely upon the works of such writers as A. J. Villiers, Frank Bowen, and Captain A. G. Course; while more than once my memory has been jogged by some article or reference or picture in *Sea Breezes*, or by a name in one of the priceless Crew Lists which are housed in the County Archives.

Above all, I am indebted to my mother who, before her death in 1964, gave me precious nuggets of information about the seven years which she spent at sea, and so enabled me to have a general picture of what life aboard a three-masted barque was like in the years before the first World War. Invaluable also have been some notes and letter written by her at odd times. They were not compiled systematically or with a view to possible publication, for at no time did she consider writing an account of her experiences, her argument being that they were in no way exceptional, but more than once she was prevailed upon to give a talk to some local society or other, and some of the notes which she used on such occasions have survived. Another mine of detailed information is a letter which she wrote in September 1940, when I had been invited to give the Pontypool Rotary Club a talk on 'Seamen of North Wales' and had sent her a frantic cry for help. Her reply has enabled me to fill in many spaces which would otherwise have remained blank.

My heartfelt thanks are also due to Mr Bryn Parry, the County Archivist, for his unfailing help and counsel, and for the good-humoured patience which he showed in coping with the problems of publication; to the members of his staff, for so consistently demonstrating that it is possible to combine charm with efficiency; and to Mr Aled Eames, without whose encouragement this book would not have been thought of, let alone seen the light of day.

The Setting

Those who know Nefyn will not need to be told that it is one of the most attractive spots in Gwynedd, with an eventful history which goes back over many centuries.

In the words of the Royal Commission on Ancient Monuments: 'Nefyn stands on fairly level ground at about 100 feet O.D., roughly a quarter of a mile from the sheltered bay which forms the natural harbour of Porth Nefyn. The greater part of the area is pasture, mostly low-lying but backed on the South East by Garn Boduan and adjacent hills'. Some 14 miles to the South West is Aberdaron, 21 miles to the North East Caernarfon, 7 miles to the South Pwllheli, and 30 miles to the North (across the waters of Caernarfon Bay) Holyhead.

No one knows at what precise stage in its history this spot was first occupied or became the site of a permanent settlement. The evidence available is interesting but inconclusive. Not far from the summit of Garn Boduan (900 feet above O.D.) are the remains of circular stone huts which date from the early days of Roman Britain, and on the summit itself the foundations of much older huts which suggest that a large hillfort existed there long before the Romans arrived. But beyond the period covered by such evidence lies an area of pure speculation.

The first recorded reference to Nefyn as a port appears in the latter half of the 11th century, when it began to figure in the plans of the Welsh prince Gruffydd ap Cynan. On his frequent journeys by boat from North Wales to Dublin, Gruffydd used Abermenai as his home base, but, whenever the wind on his return voyage blocked his approach to the Straits, he found Nefyn a convenient refuge. Countless other sailors since then have made the same discovery.

Another century was to elapse before Gerald the Welshman passed through Nefyn in 1188 on his famous pilgrimage from South Wales to Bardsey. By then the area inland from Porth Nefyn constituted one of the largest manors of the princes of Gwynedd, and within that manor was a small but flourishing market town, recognised by everyone as the dominant commercial and administrative centre in Lleyn. It also included a Priory where Gerald spent the night as guest of the Prior, and incidentally discovered a unique coloured manuscript of the Life of Merlin. Not far from the Priory, the Welsh princes had built what is described as a 'plas'; not a palace in the modern sense, but still an impressive residence, with a hall and gallery, which enjoyed the status of being the principal royal seat in Lleyn. In the neighbouring town of Pwllheli was a royal hunting lodge.

Under the Normans, Nefyn was listed as one of the 4 chief ports in the county, along with Caernarfon, Conwy, and Pwllheli. The main local industry was herring-fishing, but the townspeople must already have learned from experience that herring shoals could be fickle in their movements, and it was presumably as a form of insurance against such fickleness that they took care to invest in the land as well as in the sea. Most of them might fairly be described either as modest tenant farmers who owned a share in boats and nets, or else as fishermen who reared animals and cultivated plots of land on the side. Rent records of the period indicate the dual nature of the life which they led, together with the varying degrees of prosperity which they achieved. Whereas one man might have to be content with 1 cow and 1 net, his neighbour might be the proud owner of 4 oxen, 1 cow, 1 heifer, 1 horse, 1 boat and 4 nets.

In 1284 King Edward I arranged what has been called 'a midsummer pageant at the royal seat of Nefyn'. This took the form of a tournament which was held in Cae Iorwerth and was attended by the nobility of the country and by many foreign guests. It was modelled upon the Round Table, and no expense was spared to convince the spectators that, in the person of Edward I, Britain had found a second King Arthur. Not everything went according to plan. As one chronicler records, the wooden floor of a marquee where a ball was being held collapsed under the weight of the dancers.

Three generations later, in 1349, King Edward's great-grandson the Black Prince formally granted Nefyn the status of a Free Borough, a distinction which it enjoyed for well over 500 years. But such conspicuous marks of royal favour did not pass un-noticed, and in the year 1400 came retribution. Some of the supporters of Owain Glyndŵr convinced themselves that the burgesses of Nefyn were far too amicably disposed towards the English, and showed their displeasure by devastating the town. Every single building was burned to the ground and the manor lands laid waste. So thoroughly was the work carried out that, almost 20 year later, long after Owain Glyndŵr had retired from the field and hostilities were over, the borough was completely deserted and shunned by everyone as a ghost town of ill omen. Its former prosperity and predominance had become things of the past, and it was only slowly and painfully that it struggled back to life and became the home of a new community. In many respects it never fully recovered from its temporary extinction, and the Royal Commissioners on Ancient Monuments sadly record that 'the parish contains no important monuments'.

During its second lease of life, the sea remained all-important in the local economy, and by the end of the 16th century a brisk trade had developed between Nefyn and Pwllheli on the one hand, and the Cheshire and Lancashire ports on the other. Herring was carried on the outward journey, and corn and salt on the way back. Those trading limits were gradually extended to include ports like Dublin, Milford Haven, and Carlisle. In 1747, according to Lewis Morris who at that time was Excise Officer for Beaumaris and Holyhead, 5,000 barrels of salted fish were sent abroad from Nefyn, '*heb sôn am yr hyn a fwytawyd yn y wlad hon*'. It was during this period that herring came to be referred to as 'Nefyn beef'.

Despite such prosperity, the fishermen of Nefyn had not forgotten the lessons of the past and still felt the need to buttress themselves against fate by seeking some alternative source of revenue. High on their list of alternatives was smuggling, which reached its peak in the area some 200 years ago. Their activities in this direction were helped by the nature of the Lleyn coastline, which made the life of the local Excise Officer extremely arduous, and at times impossible. Not infrequently there were open clashes between the smugglers and the forces of law and order, and a special Report in 1726 mentions serious rioting in the borough. But, as time went on, the offenders found that less violent methods could achieve more satisfactory results. Once, in 1791, when two Excise Officers in Portinllaen boarded a smugglers' ship to investigate, they were welcomed abroad with due deference and then quietly locked in the cabin for 5 hours while the goods were discharged, and finally released only when the ship was ready to sail. On another day, 4 ships with contraband aboard deliberately arrived in the bay together and so presented the authorities with a 4-pronged dilemma.

Typical instances of this kind suggest that, for the officers of the Crown, Portinllaen in the 18th century must have been a source of acute and constant embarrassment. For local seamen it must have proved a fertile hot-bed of initiative and resourcefulness.

Since the men of Nefyn had long been in the habit of building their own boats, it was natural that sooner or later they should have turned their attention to the building of ships. This comparatively late development may be traced from the early years of the last 19th century. What gave it a special impetus was the upsurge in the slate industry and the concurrent growth of ship-building in Porthmadog and Pwllheli. In the years between 1810 and 1880, 191 small ships of varying tonnage were built on Nefyn beach.

During this building boom, more than one shipping company was formed in the borough, and all those residents who had money to spare jumped at the invitation to become shareholders. Of the individual ship-builders one of the best known was John John Thomas, sometimes referred to as 'brenin Nefyn'. At one stage he was reputed to have 300 carpenters on his pay-roll; and although this figure is probably exaggerated, there can be no doubt that he was a highly successful operator. He was also highly energetic, for once every week he walked over the Rivals to collect his workmen's wages from the Bank in Caernarfon.

Parallel with the growth of shipbuilding in Nefyn there came naturally enough a comparable change in the outlook and attitude of local seamen. They ceased to think in terms of short voyages to Merseyside and elsewhere on this side of the Irish Sea, with Dublin on the other side as the most exotic port of call, and began to look towards other, more distant horizons. In order to satisfy this new craving, some of them served their apprenticeship aboard the sloops and schooners plying between Porthmadog and the Baltic, or Newfoundland, or the Dutch West Indies, before graduating to the larger schooners, the barques, and the full-riggers which sailed from the major British ports to Australia, the Far East and the Americas. Others dispensed with the preliminaries and became Cape-Horners in one stride. Some started at the age of 12, and signed on for a first voyage which might last for anything up to three years.

A visitor to Nefyn midway through the last century would have found a bustling little community of sailors, ship-builders and ship-owners, sail-makers, nailers, carpenters, and rope-winders. He would have noticed that it was also a buoyant community, with a quiet confidence based upon past achievements and future prospects. It was among such people that, in the year 1865, my father was born.

1

Roots

My mother was not a native of Nefyn, and neither of her parents had any family links with Lleyn. Her father John Owen was born in Llanfairfechan in 1857, and her mother Miriam Roberts in Penmaenmawr later in the same year. It was not until 1905 that they and their children came to Nefyn to live, and there is no reason to suppose that they had any previous connection with the place.

The Owen family had its roots firmly fixed in Anglesey, by all accounts in the Parish of Penmynydd. One notable relative was Richard Owen of Ystum Werddon, Llangristiolus, who became famous in the 1870s as 'Richard Owen y Diwygiwr'. But the family historians also insist that there is a much earlier connection, through both parents of Richard Owen, with a character known as 'Robert y Cowper', who played a conspicuous role as one of the pioneers of Methodism in Anglesey.

During the first half of the 18th century most parishes on the island had a sprinkling of enthusiastic Methodists who, like their co-religionists in other parts of the country, had to be content with the services of itinerant preachers who delivered their homilies either in the open air or in private houses. The owners of those houses needed to be men of rare courage, for they risked having to face the wrath of both the established Church and the secular authorities. In the parish of Llangristiolus the first man to lend his home for such a purpose was 'Robert y Cowper', who then lived at Bryn-y-gors-bach, and whose life was divided into two starkly contrasting halves.

During his youth in the Trefdraeth area his way of life delighted the rabble but was the despair of his parents and of all right-minded folk. He revelled in cock-fighting and gained a reputation as a prize-fighter. Above all, as a football player he was feared by everyone for his speed and uncompromising ferocity. But one Sunday afternoon, in a particularly vicious encounter near Malltraeth Cob, he broke a thigh. Recognising this set-back as an act of God, he realised in a flash the folly of his ways and turned his back for ever on his former pursuits. From then on he applied himself assiduously to good works, and by his example and exhortation gained so many converts to the Methodist cause that in 1764 a chapel (the first of its kind on the island) had to be built to accommodate the congregation.

Had 'Robert y Cowper' lived for another 100 years, he would have approved of 'Richard Owen y Diwygiwr' as an authentic chip off the old block. It would have grieved him to know that my grandfather's branch of the family were staunch Congregationalists.

It was probably some time in the early 1840s that Taid's father, Charles Owen, crossed the Menai Straits to the Llanfairfechan area to work on the railway which was then being built along the North Wales coast as part of the line linking London with Holyhead. When that project was completed in 1848, he found fresh employment as a 'miner' in the local granite quarry overlooking both the railway and the sea. Within a few years he also found a wife, settled in Llanfairfechan, and became the head of a large family comprising one daughter and five sons, of whom Taid was the eldest.

As a miner, his job was to drill holes in the rock face, place charges of dynamite, and produce the explosion necessary to provide the stone-masons with the raw material of their craft. In the course of his duties he lost one eye and one leg. But such accidents did not deter his sons, who, when they were old enough to wield a hammer, joined him on Penmaenmawr mountain.

It was not an easy life, for, although the Pen quarry owners were among the most enlightened of their day, working conditions on the high open rock were inevitably harsh; and although the railway had brought prosperity to the quarry by providing it with a convenient and relatively cheap form of transport, there were still periods, especially in winter, when work was scarce. During such lean spells the quarrymen followed the common practice of going to America for 18 months or so at a time.

Their favourite haunt was Red Granite, a small township a few miles from Berlin, Wisconsin, where there was already a large Welsh contingent. Some of them stayed to become American citizens, and their descendants are still to be found there, while the distinctive culture which they fostered survives in such names as 'Welsh District', 'Evans College' (Ripon) etc. By today the old quarry in Red Granite is no more than a vast hole in the ground, and, being conveniently full of water, provides a happy hunting ground for skin divers.

There were times when Taid made oblique references to his American visits, usually with a smile on his face, and there is no doubt that I should have questioned him more closely and listened more attentively to what he had to say. Unfortunately I did not. What I am left with is the general impression that the barracks in which they were billeted must have looked like a shanty-town in the Klondyke during the Gold Rush, and that the standard form of relaxation for the men was to attend barn-dances where the music was provided by itinerants fiddlers and the MC's favourite command was 'Ladies in the centre; all take a dance!'

His last trip to Red Granite was made in 1892, by which

time he was a married man of about 35 with a growing family. It was in September 1892 that Gentleman Jim Corbett defied the odds by winning the world's heavyweight title from John L. Sullivan, and Taid spoke almost with awe of the excitement which swept the country for weeks before and after that historic event.

Of his brothers, the nearest to him in age and appearance was Hugh. Like Taid, Hugh had blue eyes and sandy hair; he also had two hobbies at which he excelled – singing and fighting. They were not unmixed blessings. His tenor voice made him widely popular in concerts and other convivial gatherings, but, like so many singers before and since, he sometimes developed a thirst which he found it difficult to slake. And although his straight left gained him a few welcome dollars in fair-grounds and boxing-booths, it was also liable to erupt under pressure in the wrong place or at the wrong time.

It is one of my many regrets that I never met Uncle Hugh. By the time that I had grown old enough to be aware of his existence, he had married a lady from Trefor called Cordelia Cooke and emigrated to California, where some of his children are still alive. The only other survivors among Taid's siblings were a sister who lived in San Rafael, on the outskirts of San Francisco, and a brother William in Llanfairfechan.

Nain's family (Roberts) lived for some generations in Ro-wen in the Conwy Valley before moving closer to the quarry at Penmaenmawr. Numerous descendants of the clan still inhabit the area. One of Nain's cousins was Gwylfa Roberts, a well-known poet-preacher who from 1898 until 1935 served as minister of the 'Tabernacl' Congregational chapel in Llanelli. He twice won the Crown at the Welsh National Eisteddfod. Mother was with him when he won at Blaenau Ffestiniog in 1898 and she was quite un-nerved when he stood up after the adjudication. Those Llanelli people who are old enough to have known him speak of him with deep affection and respect. I remember him as a good preacher with a pleasant voice who invariably had something interesting to say, and as a delightfully unpretentious companion.

My grandparents were married in 1877, at the age of 20. As Taid by then had found work in the quarry overlooking the village of Trefor, they spent a few months in lodgings at Llanaelhaearn before making their home in Llithfaen, For a while they were accompanied by Uncle Hugh, who was lucky enough to be able to indulge his artistic and martial tastes alike by joining the Band of the local Militia. Both he and Taid were built on large lines, and until recently many Llithfaen people could recall what a fine sight the two brothers made as they returned home on summer evenings, striding briskly along the rough path which still runs from the quarry to Llithfaen above Nant Gwrtheyrn.

During their stay in Llithfaen the Owens had 9 children – John (who died shortly after birth), Grace (my mother), Naomi, John Richard, Phoebe, Miriam, Myfanwy, Enid, and Idris. When the time came for them to attend the village school, its headmaster was Mr Griffith, who had an almost exclusive passion for music. Thanks to him, all the Owen children found that playing the piano or the harmonium, either by ear or from a score, was no more difficult than reading a book.

When my mother was 13, she became first a Monitor and then a Pupil Teacher at the school. She did not have a Secondary School education for the simple reason that, when such a school was established at Pwllheli in 1895, she was officially too old to be admitted; but six years later (1901-2) she spent a session at the University College of North Wales in Bangor, following the so-called 'Normal' course and gaining the equivalent of what is now called a 'Dip. Ed.'. Her probationary year as a teacher (1902-3) was spent in the Borough, London.

* * *

My father's parents were both of Nefyn stock, their two families having been established in the area for generations and produced the usual crop of sailors. According to the family Bible, they were married in Caernarfon. The incomplete entry reads:

> 'Hugh Davies, born at Fron, Nevin, on the   day of 1831, was married to Ellin Davies, Penrallt, Nevin, on the 8th day of July 1861 at Llanbeblig Church, Carnarvonshire. Ellin Davies, wife of Hugh Davies, was born on the 23rd day of May 1836'.

They began their married life in Victoria Terrace, Well Street, two doors away from the well which gives the street its name. In that house five children were born. The first, a boy called William, died soon after reaching his first birthday, but the other four survived – a second William (my father), John, Jane Mary, and Annie Verona.

Both Hugh and Ellin Davies died in early middle age, and on William, as the oldest surviving member of the family, fell the responsibility of keeping the home intact. In the early years such a task would have been far beyond him but for the generous help which he received from friends, relatives, and neighbours in both Nefyn and Morfa.

He left home to go to sea in 1879 at the age of 14, and one of his earliest memories was of running into foul weather and of feeling so sick that, when his turn came to work the pump, he had to be lashed to it – a simple remedy which he found more effective than any words of sympathy.

About two year later his brother John followed his example, only to make the sickening discovery that he was colour-blind, which permanently barred the road to promotion. He therefore decided to abandon the sea, and, when the opportunity came, he jumped ship in Melbourne, found a job there in a shipping office, and made that city his home for the rest of his life. He married an Australian wife, became the father of three children, and lived comfortably in a suburban house called 'Nevin Cottage'. He and Father remained firm friends and met at intervals during the years to come, but I sensed sometimes that his two sisters, although they corresponded regularly with him, never wholly forgave him for so abruptly breaking his family ties. He was, so to speak, the Prodigal Son who may have repented but never came back, and as such compared unfavourably with the elder son who had stood his ground in the evil days and kept the home fires burning.

2

1879-1903

Without ever consciously thinking about it, I had always assumed that Father's first ship was the *Eivion*. Certainly no earlier ship was ever mentioned in my hearing. But a study of the Crew Lists suggests that I was mistaken, and, although the evidence is flimsy and even misleading, there are grounds for believing that he may have shared at least part of the period 1879-84 between the *Arabella* and the *Queen of Cambria*.

(We now know, thanks to Gwerfyl Gregory of Amgueddfa Forwrol Llŷn, Nefyn's impressive Maritime Museum housed in the old St Mary's Church, that he had in fact served on the *Agnes* between 28th March and 23rd June 1881. The *List of Testimonials and Statement of Service at Sea* which Gwerfyl had unearthed also shows that he then served on the *Unicorn* for exactly a year from 9th February 1882. He subsequently sailed on the *Arabella* for nearly ten months in 1883, followed by fifteen months on board the *Queen of Cambria* from January 1884 before joining the *Eivion* in July 1885.)

The *Arabella* was a small wooden, carvel-built brigantine of 135 tons launched in 1871. Her owner was William Lloyd, Chandler, of High Street, Portmadoc, and most of the Welsh members of her crew were regularly drawn from that area. Her original Articles describe her as 'Foreign Going Ship', but in practice she sailed no further than Madeira or the Mediterranean or the Baltic, and from 1874 until her demise in 1886 she was listed as being 'for Home Trade only'.

The *Queen of Cambria* was a much more solid vessel, being an iron 3-masted barque of 834/888 tons, built at Hylton in 1876 for William Thomas of Bodlondeb, Nefyn, and registered at Caernarfon. For 30 years she sailed to Australasia and the Far East, made frequent roundings of Cape Horn in both directions, and kept on threading her way successfully through the hazards of the west coast of South America. For most of her life her Master was Moses Parry of Pwllheli, who also owned 4 of the 64 shares invested in her. The other 13 shareholders included: Robert Rees of Penllel, Nefyn; Richard Owen of Mynyddednyfed, Criccieth; three 'Ministers of the Gospel' (John Evans of Treborth, William Richard Jones of Llanrwst, Owen Charles Evans of Rhyl); and a certain Robert Thomas of No. 1 Marine Terrace, Criccieth, described simply as 'Commercial Traveller'.

Robert Thomas was a native of Nefyn. He had a brother, John, who by all accounts hardly strayed beyond the sound of the parish church bells, and whom I dimly remember as an elderly man who lived in Tai'r Lôn and was apparently content to own a cow and a narrow strip of grazing land. Robert had other ideas. After a short spell as Pupil Teacher in the Nefyn Board School, he went to Liverpool to seek his fortune. By 1876, as we have seen, he was a share-holder in the *Queen of Cambria*: within a few years he was in a position to buy the vessel for himself and add her to what was to become one of the best known fleets in North Wales, flying the ensign of Messrs. Robert Thomas & Co. of Liverpool and Criccieth.

Both the *Arabella* and the *Queen of Cambria* came to a sad end. On the 14th October 1886 the former became a total loss off the eastern seaboard of Spain, a few miles north of Barcelona, and her epitaph was written in Spanish, for the final entry in her Log is an account of the disaster as seen through the eyes of the Alcaldia Constitucional at San Filieu de Guixols . . . Twenty years later the *Queen of Cambria*'s good luck also ran out, when His Britannic Majesty's Consul at Callao regretfully informed her owners that she had struck a submerged rock at Lobes de Tierra Island and become a total wreck.

How much time Father spent on the *Queen of Cambria* or *Arabella* is a matter of conjecture. What is certain is that at Sharpness in July 1885 he joined the *Eivion*, a 3-masted barque of 1133/67 tons built at Hylton in 1879 for the North Wales Shipping Company, Nefyn, and registered at Caernarfon. Belonging to the same company was the ship *Gwynedd* of 1,953 tons, built in 1877. The Managing Owner of the two vessels was William Thomas of Bodlondeb, who has already been mentioned as owner of the *Queen of Cambria* and who acted as Secretary of the North Wales Shipping Company. Unfortunately, this company drifted into financial difficulties and, after a series of commercial experiments which proved abortive, sold its two ships to Messrs. Robert Thomas & Co.

When Father became a member of the *Eivion* crew, she was six years old and had known only one Master, Evan Jones, whose address is given variously as 'Liverpool' or as 'Talafon, near Pwllheli'. Her three Officers – Mate Henry Parry, Second Mate John Williams, Third Mate William Thomas – were from Nefyn. This presumably had the effect of making Father fell very much at home.

For some time he must have been thinking of his career in terms of promotion, and, whenever he came home between voyages, much of his time was spent at the small private school run by Hugh Davies the Nailer, who taught scores of young seamen the elements of Navigation and Plane Geometry so that they could cope successfully with the Board of Trade examinations. One of Father's classmates was Hugh Davies's son Evan, who later became widely known as Master of such White Star liners as the *Baltic* and the *Athentic*.

The effects of Hugh Davies's tuition became apparent soon after Father joined the *Eivion*. For his first trip, which lasted 15 months and took in Melbourne, Valparaiso, Pisagua, Rotterdam, and Cardiff, he had signed on as Able Seaman. For the next one – Monte Video, Valparaiso, Iquique, and Leith – he served as Second Mate, and on arrival home was immediately promoted Mate. This proved to be Captain Evan Jones's last voyage on the *Eivion*, and at Leith he was succeeded by Father's uncle and name-sake, William Davies of Boduan, later of 'Islwyn', Nefyn, whose connexion with her was to last, with one short break, for 16 years. During the first six years of that spell, uncle and nephew collaborated happily as Master and Mate until, at the end of 1893, illness or some other consideration prompted William Davies senior to miss a voyage, and he was temporarily 'superseded' by Father, who thus assumed his first independent command in January 1894. Whatever the precise circumstances, it must have been an exciting moment for him when, on the eve of sailing from Liverpool, he appended his signature for the first time to a declaration that 'All discharges and engagements have been duly made with my crew at this port in conformity with the Merchant Shipping Acts'. Their first port of call was Buenos Aires, where six hands deserted, and 11 months later they returned via Queenstown to Hull.

During his 9-year stint aboard the *Eivion*, Father was joined from time to time by some of his closest friends. One was his cousin Elias Davies, who served both as Bosun and as Sailmaker; another was Daniel Evans of 'Tynllys', who happened to meet him one Spring day on the quay in Caernarvon and was easily persuaded to sign on as an

Oridnary Seaman for his first blue-water trip. Captain Dan Evans was eventually to become an eminent figure in maritime circles and spent many of the inter-war years as Shore Superintendent for Elder Dempster in New York. There he was joined by his family, with the result that his three children – Niel, Mair, and William – received most, if not all, of their higher education in the USA. Niel, for instance, started his formal studies by my side in the Nefyn Council School but completed them at the University of Princeton, where he graduated with Honours in Civil Engineering.

It was at the end of 1894 that Father left the *Eivion* for the *Gwrtheyrn Castle*, another 3-masted barque of 777/797 tons registered at Caernarvon. She was then 18 years old, having been built at Hylton in 1876 for Robert Rees of Penllel who owned 28 of her 64 shares. The remaining 36 shares were distributed equally between William Owen of Portmadoc (her Master on her maiden voyage), William Jones (Farmer) of Clynnog, and Edmund Jones (Farmer) of Llandwrog. In January 1877, on her return from her maiden voyage, Robert Rees sold 12 of his 28 shares to Robert Davies of Tyddyncoed, Boduan, who then succeeded William Owen as Master.

Her crew normally consisted of a Mate, Second Mate or Bosun, Carpenter, Steward, Cook, Sailmaker, 5 Able Seamen and 1 Ordinary Seaman. With a complement of '14 persons all told' she was considered to be 'fully manned'. It is noticeable that, despite her connexion with Nefyn, only a handful of local men served on her before the mast. They included Elias Davies who, as he did on the *Eivion*, filled the roles of both Bosun and Sailmaker; John Lloyd 'Moorings' who made one trip in 1885-6 at the age of 19 and was to end his career as Shore Superintendent in Monte Video; John Jones 'Tawelfa', a well-known Cook and local character who had already deployed his skills on a number of other ships including the *Queen of Cambria* and the *Western Monarch*; and William Wilson, who signed on as an Able Seaman in 1879, and who five years later was to rejoin her as Master.

On the other hand, the Gwrtheyrn had an almost unbroken succession of Masters and Officers from the Nefyn area – Robert Davies, Richard Davies, John Parry, William Wilson, my father – who, between them, covered the quarter century from 1877 to 1903, the only break in that sequence coming in 1889-92 when the Master was an Englishman from Liverpool called William Hansord.

All Master Mariners were by definition expected to be able to look danger in the eye without becoming unduly excited, but Captain Hansord seems to have been an uncommonly cool customer, as is well illustrated by an episode in which he became involved some three years after leaving the *Gwrtheyrn*. By then he was Master of the *Cambrian King*, a ship of 1,638 tons belonging to the famous Cambrian Line owned by Captain Thomas Williams of Parciau, Criccieth. Mrs Hansord and her infant daughter were also aboard... In March 1897, on their way from New York with a cargo of case oil for Shanghai, they ran into a hurricane which they were lucky to survive, for in the course of it the French full-rigger *Villen De Saint Nazaire* went to the bottom with all hands, and forty ships in all were reported missing. It was in the small hours of March 4th that the first gusts caught the *Cambrian King*, with such ferocity that she heeled over on to her beam ends; her cargo shifted, and she lay helpless with water up to her hatches. As the weather worsened, it was decided to cut away her yardarms; before long it became evident that, if she were to stand a chance of surviving, her masts too must go. The crew were about to tackle this task when, without warning, the wind veered sharply from South to South-west, with almost miraculous results, for the vessel stood up, righted herself, and although stripped bare, set off before the wind... At one stage Mrs Hansord and her child were isolated in the stateroom, the door jammed by the pressure of pounding seas, and, as the water came up to her armpits, she was reduced to holding her child at arm's length above her head. Eventually she was dragged through the skylight to the comparative safety of the poop... The ship suffered such damage that the subsequent bill for repairs came to nearly 30,000 dollars. In the official report which Captain Hansord drafted for the owners, he referred in passing to his wife's ordeal, adding the mild comment: 'It was valuable experience; it proved that she had no fear so long as she knew that I was doing my best.' As a laconic under-statement this surely deserves to rank with the message which Messrs. Lawthers of Belfast once received in the mid-1850s from one of their Masters: 'The only event I have to report is that the ship struck a reef and is a total loss.'

Coolness and restraint in the face of adversity were not the only virtues taken for granted in a shipmaster, who was also expected to show the wisdom of Solomon in coping with the innumerable problems which bedevilled life at sea. Somehow or other he had to devise ways and means of handling a motley collection of men under conditions which at best were trying and at their worst sub-human.

Food, e.g., was always a likely source of complaint, and a perfect gift to potential trouble-makers. The highest compliment that any sailor could pay a shipping company was to say that it had 'well-found ships in sails, tackle, and grub'; but, unfortunately, not all owners and agents and Masters were either as conscientious or as wise as they might be. The Board of Trade had laid down clear guidelines as to how crews were to be fed, and a typical scale of provisions for a vessel with a crew of 14/15 might read as follows:

Salt Beef – 1½ lb four days a week.   Biscuits – 1 lb daily
Salt Pork – 1¼ lb three days a week. Tea – ⅛ oz daily
Flour – ½ lb three days a week.   Coffee – ½ oz daily
Peas – ⅓ pint three days a week.   Sugar – 14 oz per week
Rice – ½ lb one day a week
Water – 3 quarts daily (for Cooking, Washing & Drinking).

On short outings, such as crossing the Channel or the North Sea in tow, those detailed instructions were replaced by a general statement of the need to provide 'sufficient without waste', but on all voyages of any duration the official standards applied, and no individual concerned with the victualling of a British ship could be in any doubt as to his legal and moral duty. Equally unambiguous was the stern injunction that 'no grog' should be allowed aboard.

Human nature being what is is, the regulations were often ignored, when owners and middle-men attached more importance to the lining of their own pockets than to the welfare of their men. On the best of ships the constant diet of 'salted horse and pea-soup' could be grindingly monotonous; on the worst the tack could vary from the merely unpalatable to the unspeakably rancid. Add to such trials the fact that the men's quarters might have no heat or ventilation, that the half-deck was often awash and the space in the fo'c's'le further reduced by having the anchor chain passing through, and there is a classic recipe for mutiny on the highs seas. The miracle is that trouble did not flare up oftener than it did. What kept it within manageable bounds was the simple fact that for most seamen the mysterious spell cast by the sea overshadowed all other considerations and made the threshold of their tolerance abnormally high.

They were equally philosophical about their wages. On a barque like the *Gwrtheyrn* the crew's monthly rates of pay could be:

Mate: £6 to £6.10.0;
2nd Mate: £4 to £4.10.0;
Bosun: £3.5.0;
Cook/Steward: £4.15.0;
Carpenter & Sailmaker: £4.10.0 to £5;
A.B.: £2/1-/- tp £3/5/0;
O.S.: £1 to £2.5.0;
Boy: 10/-.

In addition to the problems of food and accommodation, there were other potential sources of trouble that a Master had to guard against. Not least of these was the possibility, and even the likelihood, that most members of his crew might be foreigners, with only a quaint smattering of English. In such a context language became a burning issue, and he was often compelled to rely for guidance upon the intelligence and good will of some crew member who might be both able and willing to play the role of interpreter. Only by some such arrangement could an acceptable degree of peace and harmony he preserved aboard; and, if the arrangement broke down, the misunderstanding which followed could quickly fester into disconetent, resentment, and worse. Even a cursory reading of the Crew Lists suggests that the arrangement did not always work. When one considers the obvious implications, one may begin to realise the immense weight of responsibility carried by a shipmaster, and the equally immense relief he must have felt every time that his ship sailed safely into harbour.

Many of Father's friends have told me that one of his great virtues was his ability to pick a good crew. He was a shrewd judge of human nature and, given any choice, generally managed to surround himself with men whom he could rely upon for loyal service. Sometimes, like everybody else, he made mistakes; sometimes he had no choice but to sign on some of the riff-raff who haunted the larger ports and drifted more or less aimlessly from ship to ship. He had met some of these characters before leaving the *Eivion*; he was soon to meet some more.

The voyages of the *Gwrtheyrn* naturally varied in length, from a minimum of 9/10 months to a maximum of 3 years. The first 3 after Father joined her were relativey short, the third (in 1896) being a typical run from Liverpool to Rio, then westward round the Horn to Lota, before returning eastward round the Horn to Dublin. The fourth voyage was on ampler lines, from Dublin to Swansea, Mauritius, Rangoon, Rio de Janeiro, Talcahuano, Taltal, Melbourne, Newcastle NSW, and a final rounding of the Horn to Antwerp. The 3 years which that voyage occupied were not without incident. Of the 32 men whose names appear on the Crew List, 5 signed on in Dublin, 7 in Swansea, 2 in Rangoon, 1 in Latitude 19 S. by Longitude 13 W., 1 in Rio, 7 in Melbourne, 4 in Newcastle NSW, and 5 in Callao. Most of these changes in personnel occurred in the ordinary way as individual hands were discharged and paid off 'by mutual consent', but one seaman was lost because he failed to report for duty, two were taken ill and had to be left in hospital, while four deserted in Callao.

Almost as long and as chequered was Father's last voyage with her. On this round trip of 2½ years – from February 1901 until July 1903 – both the Mate and the Cook came from Nefyn, and the Second Mate from Penygroes, but the rest of the crew consisted of 1 Russian Finn, 3 Americans, 2 Swedes, 1 Norwegian, and 2 Irishmen of no fixed abode but claiming to have some connection (unspecified) with the Rue de la Culotte Bleue in Dublin. With such a mixed brew, some degree of instability was likely, if not inevitable, as the details of the Log show. They sailed from Liverpool to Brisbane (where 8 deserted), Newcastle NSW, Mauritius (1 deserted), Sydney (1 deserted), Cape Town, Sydney, Newcastle NSW (1 deserted), Coquimbo to the North of Valparaiso, Pisagua (1 deserted). The homeward run round Cape Horn brought them to Falmouth, Rotterdam, Antwerp, and Liverpool.

Although Father left her in 1903 to join the *Gwydyr Castle*, he always looked back with pleasure on the nine years spent aboard the *Gwrtheyrn*. Had he been able to foresee what was to happen to her, he might have been saddened by what he saw, for during a life-span of more than half a century that attractive and durable little barque had what can best be described as a varied career. After 33 years' service in British hands – first for her original owner Robert Rees and then for Robert Thomas – she was sold in 1909 to the Italians. They in turn passed her on in 1918 to the Finns, who re-christened her *Ira* and used her for the next two years in the Baltic timber trade. The Norwegians then bought her, but they too disposed of her in 1923, and, when last sighted and reported in 1929, she was a hulk in Sydney harbour.

In 1903, however, she was still in active unit of the Robert Thomas fleet and had over 25 more years to go. The ill-fated *Eivion* proved less durable. She remained in service until 1904, when her Master was Robert Thomas of 6 Corporation Terrace, Criccieth. Her Mate also was from Criccieth, her Second Mate from the State of Michigan, USA. Of the remaining 11 hands, 7 were Germans or Scandinavians. In addition she carried three Apprentices with ages ranging from 15 to 18. On the 10th June 1904 she left Garston bound for Valparaiso, but she never completed the voyage, for on the 3rd October, 111 days out, she caught fire and had to be abandoned. Her position before she went down was Lat. 54 S. Long. 84 W. Her crew were picked up by the full-rigged ship *Lonsdale* and landed in Valparaiso on the 17th October.

Mother must have heard of this disaster, for over a year previously she had left London and moved to Nefyn on being appointed Headmistress of the local Board School. At about the same time, by an odd coincidence, her father was made Steward of the Gwylwyr Granite Quarry – a flourishing concern in those days, but destined to be squeezed out of existence by the War. The entire Owen family therefore moved from Llithfaen to Nefyn, finding a home at 'Brynhyfryd', two doors away from Capel Soar.

When all this happened, Mother's young brother Idris Owen was 7 years old. A local custom demanded that every new boy to the district should fight each of his contemporaries in turn. Luckily for him, he was strong for his age and coped with fair success, but he also received invaluable moral support from the biggest boy in school – Evan Jones 'Penpalmant' (grandson of old John Elias the Coachman) who made a point of supervising all the fights to ensure that the newcomer had a square deal. Not so long ago I met Evan Jones, shortly after he had retired from years of service as a Crosville bus driver, and, when I reminded him of those early days, he laughed and said that he could never forget the last fight of the series. It took place one summer evening on the beach near Creigiau Bach, where an enthusiastic band of boys had gathered to egg on the gladiators. When the slugging and the subsequent hand-shaking were over, there was a general feeling that something should be done to mark the occasion. What they eventually did was to burst into song and give a spirited rendering of the verse 'O fryniau Caersalem ceir gweled' to the strains of 'Crugybar', and, as the note of that doleful melody died away among the rocks, the youngest member of the Owen family was formally integrated into his new habitat.

It was early in 1904 that my future parents met for the

first time. By then Father's salary, as Master of the *Gwydyr Castle*, had rocketed to £16 a month. In November 1905 they were married in Capel Soar by the Reverend Llewelyn Williams, much to the delight of the Board School pupils, who enjoyed both a half-holiday and a celebration tea.

3

Gwydyr Castle: Voyage 1

The *Gwydyr Castle* was a 3-masted barque of 1,512 tons, built at Dundee in 1893 by Alexander Stephens & Sons. Originally christened *Newfield*, she changed her name in 1900 on becoming the property of Robert Thomas & Co. She was famous in her day for reasons which are hinted at by Leslie Morton in *The Long Wake*: 'The next ship to us was a beautiful little barque called *Gwyder Castle*, and some of the sailors on the *Beeswing* who had shipped on her in earlier voyages told me that she sailed like a witch, and she certainly had the most beautiful underwater lines and general shape'.[1]

Morton was not the only young man to be impressed by her. In 1901 an 18-year-old Bavarian artist called Anton Otto Fischer, who had already spent 18 months in sail, signed on as a member of her crew in Hamburg, as she prepared to leave for Panama via Cape Horn. In his own words: 'Here finally was the ship of my earlier dreams, and I walked up the gang-plank and forward to the focs'le with a light step'.[2]

He felt less buoyant when they reached the Horn, for they ran into weather which he described as 'murderous', and conditions generally were so grim that he refers to them as 'two months of purgatory in a watery hell'[3] . . . He writes: 'Thinking back on those two nightmarish months it took the *Gwydyr Castle* to get round Cape Horn, I often wonder how we survived at all. It was a succession of westerly gales, the ship hove-to half the time under two lower tops'ls, making two feet south or north for every foot west; blizzards when we couldn't see 30 yards beyond the ship, and huge grey seas would loom to windward like nebulous monsters; sleet storms when rigging and footropes became coated with ice, when coiled and belayed ropes were solid blocks of ice to be pounded apart, and when sails were as stiff as boards and as unmanageable'.[4]

Her captain on this voyage was Evan Jones of Nefyn, her Mate John Owen (also of Nefyn), and her Second Mate Richard Evans of Barmouth. Fischer remained aboard for two years before signing off in New York. In that time he made several sketches which he later used as the basis for a series of oil paintings. Most of these have appeared in book form, and quite apart from their artistic merit, they have a unique documentary value, offering as they do a vivid impression of what life afloat could be like in those days of protracted voyages, cramped living quarters, capricious catering, and frayed nerves.

One picture shows the ship's steward fighting his way aft with the officers' food in the height of a roaring gale. Clutching the life-line under his left arm, he holds on to a coffee-pot in one hand and to a dish pan in the other, while the green water swirls well above his knees and threatens to sweep him off his feet . . . The subject of another picture is a fight between Fischer and a truculent Irish sailor a few days before the latter fell to his death from a yard-arm . . . A third picture depicts the burial at sea of the old sail-maker who was killed on deck one dark night when he fell and struck his head on an iron ring-bolt. He was, we are told, a Swede who had served in the Federal Navy during the American Civil War . . . In still further pictures we see a sailor being tattooed with Indian Ink . . . three seamen in the focs'le, during a lull from work, entertaining their shipmates with music from an accordeon, a mandolin, and a guitar . . . and a group of men drawing the captain's attention to a piece of meat so hard that Fischer was able to use his share of it to whittle a ship's model.

It is clear from his account that, even when the ship's general rations were not bad enough to justify a formal complaint, they still left much to be desired and at times required special treatment before becoming fit for human consumption. As he puts it: 'We would pound the hard-track into pieces and drop them in our pannikins of hot tea or coffee. In a minute or two the weevils would rise to the surface to be skimmed off'.

Fischer was paid off and left the *Gwydyr Castle* in New York late in 1903. Father joined her a few months later, and remained with her for the next 10 years. Whatever sorry tales she might have had to relate about her immediate past, he always thought of her as his favourite ship, as the fastest that he ever sailed in, the loveliest to look at, and the easiest to handle. In reasonable conditions she behaved like a yacht, especially with a good wind on her beam, when she could be expected to log 12 knots and upwards for days on end. With a following wind, strangely enough, she tended to be less lively.

It was in late November 1905 that Mother saw her for the first time. That was in Rotterdam, where she was being loaded with ballast before crossing to London to pick up a general cargo for Sydney NSW. The trip back to this country, which should have been a brief formality, produced a near-disaster, as Mother explained in a note written some years later: 'The registered tonnage of the *Gwydyr* was about 1,500, and she carried 2,250 tons. For ballast she required 750 tons, as she had a very sharp bottom. Thinking to economise, an overseer in Rotterdam only put in 550 tons for the short tow to London. As it was midwinter, a heavy squall sprang up in the North Sea and the vessel capsized. Needless to say, the man responsible was frightened almost out of his wits, and it took all hands to try and trim the ballast so as to get the ship upright. This was my introduction to life at sea'.

Their berth in London for the next 3 weeks was at the West India Dock, close to Captain Scott's *Discovery* which was being groomed for one of her visits to the Antarctic. Ten days before Christmas, with their cargo safely under hatches, they were towed out on the first stage of their 3-month journey to the other side of the world.

In the Channel the weather proved reasonably friendly, but, as they entered the Bay of Biscay, they met contrary winds and tumultuous seas, with the result that it took 3 weeks to clear Cape Finistere. At one stage conditions were so bad that oil-bags had to be hung over the side in an attempt to reduce the fury of the breakers. On Christmas Day the wind howled in the rigging, and all hands stayed on deck. The effect on Mother can well be imagined. For over a fortnight, including Christmas and New Year's Day, she lay in her bunk, far too weak to lift her head from the pillows, convinced that the end must come soon, and at moments almost wishing that it would.

Beyond the Bay of Biscay the winds abated, and by the time they approached Madeira the skies were clear. Incredibly, they continued to enjoy fine weather for the rest of the trip to Australia, even when 'running the easting' in the Roaring Forties. For Mother, this meant that a trip which had threatened to develop into a nightmare was transformed into a beautiful dream.

Some 2,000 miles due west of Cape Town they sighted the island of Tristan da Cunha and hove-to so that some of the male inhabitants of the island could row out to them in their whale-boats. Each boat was piled high with fresh fruit, meat, and vegetables which their owners were anxious to barter for whatever the *Gwydyr* had to offer. The more enterprising among them made paintive requests for bottles of wine for their 'invalid wives'. Money as such meant nothing to them, but they were delighted to exchange fowl and new potatoes for flour, rice, and old clothes. Before returning ashore they left behind a parcel of letters which Father promised to post on arrival at Sydney. That night, with the help of some fat geese and fresh vegetables, supper on board the *Gwydyr* was a feast to be remembered.

Once Mother had found her sea legs, it did not take her long to settle down to the rhythm of ship life and to discover plenty of things to occupy her mind. The fact that she liked reading and sewing and knitting was obviously a help, but she soon developed additional interests. After all, she was trained to be a teacher and to take her duties seriously. As most of the apprentices and other young seamen on board were Welsh, it was only natural that she should take a maternal interest in them, and before long she had invited them to form a Bible class. Every Sunday afternoon they would meet in the captain's saloon to read and discuss some extract from the Scriptures; then would follow a session of hymn-singing around the harmonium, rounded off with tea, scones, jam, and cakes. The classes proved highly popular, although Mother had no doubt that the main attraction was the food.

98 days after leaving the Thames they reached Sydney. Mother was fast asleep in the small house when they dropped anchor quietly in one of the innumerable coves which are a distinctive feature of that magnificent harbour, and, when she woke up, the perfect stillness and the total absence of any sound apart from the singing birds on near-by trees convinced her that she must have died and landed safely in Paradise.

On their first Sunday in Sydney they attended evening service at a Welsh chapel which Father frequented whenever he was in port. The minister invited them to have supper with him and his wife, explaining that they would be joined by an old friend of his who lived some 400 miles inland but had come to town because his daughter was about to register as a student at the University of Sydney. When they met in the Manse, they were amazed to discover that the minister's friend was a cousin of Taid's whose health had broken down some 25 years previously and who had acted upon his doctor's advice to emigrate to warmer climes.

The 3 weeks which were spent unloading in Sydney enabled Mother to meet some of Father's friends and to enjoy the rich hospitality of that exuberant city. They then moved down the coast to Newcastle NSW to load coal for Valparaiso. Towards the end of May they were once more ready to sail, and, on the same day as the *Gwydyr*, 6 other ships left Newcastle bound for various South American ports. One of these 6 vanished without trace and was never seen or heard of again. The only one bound, like the *Gwydyr*, for Valparaiso was a 3-masted barque called *Ben Lee*, which took 76 days on the trip. The *Gwydyr* took 37, and, despite setbacks on the way, had almost discharged her cargo before *Ben Lee* showed up. Mother always emphasised that there could be a high degree of luck in such matters. As she put it: 'One ship might find herself becalmed in the Doldrums and yet have the mortifying experience of seeing another ship bowling merrily along about half a mile away. You might know where the wind was; getting to it was quite another matter; and more than once we had to lower boats over the side in an attempt to tow the ship, however slowly, in the general direction of the breeze.'

It was late June when they dropped anchor in Valparaiso harbour and among the first people to come aboard to greet them were Captain Davis of the *Milverton* and Captain Roberts of the *John Cooke*. They were soon followed by others whom Father knew, for the harbour was alive with about 50 sailing ships, 12 of them captained by Welshmen, of whom 4 came from Nefyn. There was nothing unusual about these figures; Mother noticed a similar proportion elsewhere on her travels.

One ship which Father was particularly glad to see was the full rigger *Kirkcudbrightshire*, with a mainly Welsh crew commanded by a close friend, David Roberts of Dolgellau. Also on board was Mrs Roberts, whom Mother now met for the first time. Thus began a firm friendship which lasted throughout their lives.

As might have been expected, it was not long before the Welsh captains arranged to meet at regular intervals, and every Sunday evening a crowd of them would congregate in the *Gwydyr*'s saloon to talk shop, exchange news, and sing hymns to the accompaniment of the old harmonium.

On the 5th July Mrs Roberts gave birth to a baby boy, and at the formal christening which took place soon afterwards Mother acted as his godmother. He was given the name of Robert David Valparaiso Roberts. In the years to come he was always known to his family and closest friends as Bob, but other friends from Dolgellau, London, and Cardiff may remember him better as Valpo.

Although the harbour at Valparaiso had much to commend it, it was generally considered to be not an ideal anchorage. The water in places was so deep that sailing ships sometimes found it impossible to lift their anchors, and, because the harbour opened to the North, ships were exposed to the full fury of the 'Northers' which swept in from time to time, often without warning. Such gales were known to cause serious damage to shipping and tragic loss of life both afloat and ashore.

Nor far from the *Gwydyr* lay the skeleton of a ship which had been the victim of a Norther a few years previously. It was pointed out to them that this was the *Foyledale* which had run aground in 1903 with only its mizzen standing. The captain was seriously injured, the rest of the crew sought refuge in the rigging, and 6 lives were lost – 2 apprentices, 2 seamen, and the captain's wife and daughter. After that storm every ship in the harbour had to be re-moored. It was during one of those heavy Northers that young Bob Roberts first saw the light of day, and extra cables had to be fixed to keep the ship from running wild.

Before the *Kirkcudbrightshire* sailed for home, the unloading of the *Gwydyr* continued at a painfully slow pace. Most of the port workers, who were of Spanish extraction and mixed blood, acted upon the principle that they should never do today what can be left until tomorrow. 'Mañana' was far and away the most popular word in their vocabulary. It soon became apparent to everyone on board that their stay in Valparaiso was unlikely to be short; and at first such a prospect was not unwelcome, since the city and its surroundings had much to offer in those days.

The main part of the city stood in the lee of a fairly high range of hills, on a tract of land reclaimed from the sea, while the suburbs extended along the crest of the hills, with steep paths connecting the lower with the higher areas. The most convenient way of climbing the heights was to use the lifts which made the journey up and down at regular intervals, but that was not the only mode of travel. One of the hills was called 'English Hill', and a popular method of spending a fine afternoon was to hire a cart drawn by three horses in order to reach the top, from where it was possible to enjoy a magnificent view of the open harbour and the ocean beyond. After returning on board, they could stand on deck and enjoy a different but equally attractive view of the land, especially at twilight, when the city was ablaze with multi-coloured lamps, and the stars shone clear above the hills.

Such idle pleasures did not last long. No more than 2 days after the *Kirkcudbrightshire* had weighed anchor and stood out to sea, all the remaining ships in harbour had the experience of living through the famous earthquake of August 1906, which shattered extensive areas of the city, killed hundreds of people, and remained like a nightmare in Mother's memory for the rest of her life.

In her own words: 'When the early tremors came and the *Gwydyr* began to shudder and creak, it was obvious that some extra disturbance was making her pull more strongly than usual on her cables. What bothered us was that there was nothing to suggest where that extra disturbance came from, since the sea was like a duck-pond and there had been no whisper of a breeze for days. We were still wondering what the explanation might be when the noise and the movements became suddenly more pronounced. The ship began to tremble like a man with a fever, so violently in fact that no one could stand without clinging to some solid support. According to the Official report which was issued later, the tremors lasted for four minutes, but it seemed more like a life-time.

'After going on deck and looking towards the shore, which was about half a mile distant, we noticed that sporadic fires were breaking out. We could also hear the cries of people and children in distress, the barking of dogs, and the distinctive sounds of other animals like cattle, horses, and mules.

'Jutting out into the harbour was a Mole, and coming from that direction were scores of rowing-boats, with the poor wretches on board screaming to be allowed to climb into the nearest ships. Since no one knew what might happen next, many of them were prepared to go anywhere, even to the open sea in their flimsy little craft, rather than return to face the horror which could be waiting for them on land.

'As the tremors continued off and on throughout the

night, sleep was out of the question, and early next day some of the men went ashore to assess the extent of the damage. They came back with heart-breaking stories. Scores of houses and other buildings were reduced to rubble, and the homeless refugees had sought shelter with their few belongings in a large public park. Some of them were astonishingly cheerful, no doubt taking the view that they were lucky to be alive. As for the disaster, they accepted that as the will of God. One enterprising young man had erected a tent as a barber's shop, with a pole outside bearing the notice: 'Barber of the Earthquake'.

'The earth tremors were followed by a period of comparative quiet, during which everyone waited for the tidal wave which regularly follows such quakes on the West Coast. For us, this meant watching the few steamers in the bay weighing anchor and heading for the open sea, while we lay there helpless, hoping for the best but dreading the worst. When the tidal wave eventually came, it took the form not of one isolated sea but of a series of seas which reared up the one behind the other like a row of houses. I counted 21 of these as they swept through the harbour in the space of a few minutes and created fresh havoc ashore. If the engineer responsible for supervising the Power House generators had not been alert enough to disconnect the electrical supply when the first wave appeared, the consequences would have been incalculably worse.

'Among scenes of such confusion it was not surprising that there should have been several cases of looting. The authorities quickly declared Martial Law and announced that any offender caught breaking the law would be executed on the spot. Many culprits were shot in the streets. There was a persistent rumour that the number killed in this summary fashion ran into thousands, but, as there had been no official census in the previous year, there was no means of checking the statistics. All that I know for certain is that the incident shattered the lives of countless innocent people, and was an ordeal that I would never willingly pass through again. Perhaps the worst part was the feeling of utter helplessness which gripped one like a paralysis.'

After three weeks of such sustained excitement, plus exposure to the hazards of cholera, typhoid, and other diseases, it was a relief to turn their backs on Valparaiso and to move on to Tocopilla to load Nitrate for home.

'A pleasant little port' are the words which Mother used to describe Tocopilla. They could hardly have applied to the general run of Nitrate centres, which were considered by those who knew them as the most desolate spots on earth. In the picture post-cards which Father sent home from time to time, towns like Talcahuano and Antofogasta have a bleakly primitive look. With their unpaved streets lined with shops and houses clustered together on high wooden sidewalks, they could well have served as models for a frontier town in the wild and woolly West; and, as one looks at the pictures, it is easy to imagine a Wells Fargo coach lurching in through a cloud of dust, or a band of desperados tearing round the nearest corner with guns blazing. Romantic perhaps, but a far cry from the 'pleasant little port' which Mother found in Tocopilla.

In fairness to the Nitrate ports, it must be said that they were not the most unpopular places on the West Coast. That dubious distinction belong to the guano islands, where the cliffs of guano towered more than 150 feet above the sea, and ships took it in turn to approach the loading bases where the guano was broken up by Chinese coolies before being sent down canvas shutes towards the waiting launches. Especially during the summer months, the heat and stench were overpowering. Worst of all was the inhuman brutality with which the coolies were sometimes treated by their guards. One report (dated 22.8.1862) reads: 'It is sickening to see them at work . . . in the hot sun, barebacks. The poor hounds had rather die than live, I believe, but they are watched too close by the Peruvian soldiers to destroy their lives now. When one dies, they throw a little guano over him, which the dogs and vultures tear up and pull to pieces. All over the graveyard may be seen heads and legs of the poor wretches'. Countless seamen, in the course of their duties, must have been sickened by such sights, and sickened even more by their impotence to do anything about it. No wonder that some of these guano islands were referred to as 'the last places that were made'.[5]

Even though the Nitrate centres had no comparable atrocities to offer, they were still far from popular with sailors. In the least attractive of them there was no harbour in the orthodox sense, only an exposed roadstead, and the task of finding a safe anchorage on some stretches of the rocky coastline was in itself fraught with danger, since strong winds could come sweeping in from the North and force a ship's crew on to a lee shore which had nothing to offer but certain disaster to a ship without engine power. Even the 'pleasant little port' of Tocopilla had its special hazards. The bay was curved like part of a circle, with a blunt headland at its northern end, and an ominous reef of sharp rocks stretching to seaward in the South. The ships in port usually lay in a single file, reaching from close under the lee of the reef to within a quarter of a mile of the headland, with only a narrow fairway between them and the shore. In rough weather, any manoeuvre was tricky, and there was no room for error.

To crown matters, at the turn of this century cartographers had not yet become sufficiently familiar with all parts of the coastline to be able to draw reliable charts, which meant that some operations had to be performed 'by guess and by God'. For a variety of good reasons, therefore, the prospect of loading Nitrate was not normally welcomed by seamen, but they were prepared to jump at it if it also offered the prospect of coming home.

Sometimes the inhabitants of the Nitrate towns would go out of their way to help by erecting directions which could be seen far out at sea. In Antofogasta, e.g., a prosperous merchant called Jose Santos Ossa, who played a leading part in establishing the town midway through the last century, took it into his head to paint on the hillside an enormous white anchor as a means of guiding ships to their moorings. He did so by employing workmen to carry a large tank to the top of the hill, and to fill it with water and lime before pouring the mixture down the slope. As the mixture began to dry in the hot sun, it was gradually moulded until it assumed roughly the shape of an inverted anchor. Since there is the minimum of rain in those latitudes, the anchor remained a conspicuous part of the landscape for years, and, for all that I know, it may still be there.

After leaving Tocopilla, Mother's worries were still not over. At the back of her mind was the knowledge that they would have to round Cape Horn, and, for one who before November 1905 had never been afloat in anything larger than a rowing dinghy, the prospect was daunting. She had heard often enough that the Horn was in a special sense the acid test in a sailor's life, since it was there that seamanship could be most violently strained, and the natural elements were at their harshest and most unpredictable.

On the 21st November 1961 the London *Times* contained an article which describes a journey past the Horn. The writer, on his way home from Australia on board the steamer *Port Pirie*, reveals his feelings as follows: 'I was in a well-found ship gliding past the Horn at 10 knots northwards and away from that terrible spot. I would not have to leave my warm bunk at midnight to climb 140 feet above the deck in pitch darkness, and stretch out on a swinging yard to battle with thrashing frozen canvas in a full gale, with only a narrow footrope between me and eternity. That is how it was for those old windjammer men of the past'. Most sailors would have agreed that, although there were other danger spots dotted in profusion all over the seven seas, there was nothing to match the unique and sinister notoriety of Cape Horn.

Of the two ways round the cape, it was generally accepted that the passage from east to west was the more exacting, because powerful headwinds added their weight to the other natural dangers to tax a crew's patience, resourcefulness and endurance to the limit, and often beyond. The longest trip that Mother ever heard of was that of the *Marathon* which left Liverpool for Valparaiso and simply disappeared. She became hopelessly overdue and was officially given up for lost. Then the owners received word from the captain who reported that he was in Australia. He had apparently met with contrary winds which made it impossible for him to round the Horn and eventually forced him to double back off course. He had put into Fremantle for repairs and supplies before proceeding to his original destination, which he reached 12 months after leaving the Mersey. On his return home he was relieved of his command ... Another ship, the *Ravenscourt*, once took 6 weeks to round the Horn on her way to a Peruvian port.

The eastward passage also had its dangers. Not the least of these was the threat of being pooped, i.e. of being overtaken and submerged by a massive sea while running before a heavy wind. In fact, from whatever direction it was approached, Cape Horn could create nasty problems for everyone.

A copy of *Sea Breezes* quotes the strange case of Captain T. Y. Powles (an old *Conway* boy) who rounded 'the dreaded Cape Stiff' 28 times during his life but 'never met with bad weather there, an unusual experience for a master mariner'.[6] Unusual indeed, for in general terms Cape Horn weather was almost invariably bad, even in summer. Although the prevailing gales from the west did not last as long in summer as in winter, they were stronger and more frequent. What made the winter so redoubtable was the fact that the winds were more variable, the cold more bitter, and the hours of daylight much reduced, lasting at most from about 9 a.m. until 3 p.m. Sometimes the difference between night and day was so blurred as to be barely perceptible, a phenomenon which John Masefield describes in lines from *The Dauber*:

'So the night passed, but then no morning broke,
Only a something showed that night was dead.'

Such an unholy combination of fogs, gigantic heaving seas, and marauding icebergs could hold up a timid ship indefinitely or cause grave damage to a bold one. The problem for captains was how to be careful without being too cautious, and the dividing line, as the master of the *Marathon* discovered to his cost, could be tragically fine.

Even with the most competent seamen in the world, things could go wrong, as happened in 1906 to the 4-masted barque *Fingal* of Dublin, when she was bound from Glasgow to Vancouver with a general cargo. 'All went well until they crossed the Line and got down into high southerly latitudes, and there, in the vicinity of the Horn, they were embayed in the ice and drifted helplessly for no less than 10 weeks, with sails furled . . . Eventually they got clear of the ice, but so frozen up was the running gear that they had to use hot water from the donkey boiler to get the ropes through the blocks'.7

This was only a few months before Mother had to face her first passage past the same dreaded spot, but by then (September 1906) the Southern winter had given place to Spring, and she saw no sign of the ice which had trapped the *Fingal* and made life so miserable for her crew. On the contrary, the *Gwydyr* enjoyed excellent weather and raced home in style.

As they approached the Cape, with a moderate wind blowing from the North, there was an incident which caused great excitement among the young apprentices and, to a lesser degree, everyone else on board. The apprentices were always eager to find themselves in a position to compete with other ships of similar rig, and at all the West Coast ports which the *Gwydyr* had visited they had been at great pains to point out to everyone within ear-shot that she was far and away the smartest thing afloat. On this particular day she was logging a steady 12/13 knots, which seemed brisk enough for ordinary purposes. They were therefore surprised to find that she was slowly being over-hauled by another 3-masted barque which, when the two ships came close enough to be able to exchange signals, proved to be the *Western Monarch*, which had once belonged to Robert Thomas & Company but was now flying the Norwegian flag.

Mother takes up the tale: 'This discovery caused great delight to the *Gwydyr* Cook, John Jones 'Tawelfa', who had made several trips on the *Western Monarch* in her Robert Thomas days and had a special place for her in his affections. But, although old loyalties die hard at sea, John Jones was now a *Gwydyr* man, and he derived no joy from watching his former love gliding remorselessly by and threatening to move out of sight. Then, just after she had moved ahead, and the *Gwydyr* apprentices were beginning to resign themselves to having to believe the unbelievable, the wind began to veer from North to North West, so that the two ships now had it on their starboard beam. For the next few days they stayed together, and you can imagine the glorious picture they made under a clear sky, with the sun shining on their white sails, and their bows plunging as the wind drove them along neck and neck. It was not until we approached the Tropics that the *Gwydyr* began to forge ahead and to show her rival a clean pair of heels.'

Although the two ships lost sight of each other for the rest of the voyage, they can never have been far apart, for, when the *Gwydyr* eventually arrived in Falmouth for orders, she was followed a few hours later on the same day by the *Western Monarch*.

The passage from Tocopilla to Falmouth, including a spell of enforced idling in the Tropics, took 96 days. On their way from Falmouth to London, they followed the standard practice of picking up a pilot off Dover for the final run through the straits and up the river. Much to Father's delight, the pilot proved to be a Captain Roberts who was a native of Nefyn and an old school friend whom Father had not seen since they were boys together. Mother's comment on the reunion was terse: 'I never heard two men talk so much in such a short space of time'.

On arrival in London they found Captain David Roberts of the *Kirkcudbrightshire* anxiously waiting for them. Mrs Roberts and the baby had already left for Dolgellau, but he wanted to know at first hand how they had weathered all the excitement in Valparaiso. Even the *Kirkcudbrightshire*, two days out from harbour, had experienced an odd turbulence which suggested that something out of the ordinary was happening somewhere.

In all, my parents had been away from home for 13 months, a comparatively short absence by the standards of those days. They reached Nefyn early in 1907, and there, in February, their first child, Ellen Gwyneth, was born.

---

[1] Leslie Morton, *The Long Wake*, p. 25. Pub. Routledge Kegan, England 1968.
[2] Oliver E. Allen and the editors of Time Life Books, *The Windjammers* (n.d.), p. 60.
[3] ibid.
[4] Katrina Sigsbee Fischer, in collaboration with Alex A. Hurst, *Anton Otto Fischer, Marine Artist, His Life and Work* (1977), p. 150.
[5] *Sea Breezes* Vol. 24, p. 235.
[6] *Sea Breezes* Vol. 4, p. 375.
[7] *Sea Breezes* Vol. 24, p. 82 ff.

*Crew of the 3-masted barque Eivion, taken in 1891/92.
The group inlcudes 5 men from Nefyn – William Davies, Isfryn (Master), my father (Mate), Hugh Jones (Second Mate), John Thomas (Purser), and Daniel Evans (Ordinary Seamen); Owen Evans (Carpenter) from Caernarfon; Owen Thomas (O.S.) from Pwllheli; a French Cook/Steward from Bordeaux; an Assistant Cook from Hamburg; one Englishman, one Belgian, and 6 Scandinavians.*

My parents on their wedding day, November 1905.

*Group taken in Godfrey's studio, Newcastle, N.S.W.
With Father are Capt. Parry of the* Thistlebank *(standing)
and Capt. Thomas of the* Maelgwyn. *[The picture is undated,
but is clearly earlier than 1905 because it was given to my mother
under her maiden name of Miss Owen].*

The 3-masted barque Gwydyr Castle.

Tomtom with my sister and myself, and one of our Melbourne cousins, aboard the Gwydyr Castle.

Father's family and that of his brother John taken together outside the latter's house in Melbourne. 1911/12.

Durban, South Africa, in March 1912.

*A characteristic group taken by Oliver Godfrey,
85 Hunter Street, Newcastle, NSW.*

My father on the poop of the Belford *in San Francisco in the summer of 1916, about to leave for home with a cargo of barley.*

July 2, 1916. A group of family friends on the poop of the Belford.

July 1916. Father with Mr P.L. Roberts and his son in the grounds of Stanford University, California.

4 July, 1916. A picnic with family friends and ship's apprentices in Golden Gate Park, San Francisco.

4

Gwydyr Castle: Voyages 2 & 3

By the 6th May they were once more on the move, accompanied by the baby, and bound as before for Sydney. By an odd coincidence, it so happens that the fullest personal account of that voyage is to be found, of all places, in a copy of the Caernarfon County School Magazine *The Arvonian*.

The issue of that magazine for December 1907 includes in its 'School Notes' the following item:

'A letter has been received from Hugh Rees, who left London some four months ago in the *Gwydyr Castle*; we are glad to know that he is getting on well and enjoying his new life.'

On his return home young Rees compiled an article which he submitted to *The Arvonian* and which duly appeared in the issue dated December 1908. It is well worth quoting in full:

'Although they say a sailor's life is bold and free, it has its disadvantages, plenty of rough work, and poor food to do it upon, but it is a very healthy life which makes one hardy, and there are not many troubles connected with it. My first voyage took a little over eighteen months. We sailed from London on May 6th 1907 for Sydney, and had several nasty blows, calms, and head winds. I did not suffer from mal de mer after the first day. After we had been out about a fortnight I happened to doze off during my watch whilst sitting on the main hatch; the Mate, whose watch I was in, whistled for me to know whether I was looking after the time or not. I, being asleep, did not hear him; after waiting a few minutes he came along to see what had become of me; he woke me up by slinging a bucket of water over me, which was a lesson for me not to sleep again during my watch.

'Thirty-one days out we passed the beautiful island of Madeira, and we ran up our numbers so that they could let them know at home that we had passed there. Forty-five days out we crossed the 'Line'; it is a day for fun on board ship when Father Neptune with his long white beard and golden crown, accompanied by his wife, comes on board and asks, 'Have you ever crossed the Line before?' Those who have not done so have always to be shaved by Father Neptune's assistant barber. A mixture of paint and dirty fluid is made into a sort of paste and slabbed on one's face, and as much as possible put into one's mouth if one does not keep it closed – then the paint is scraped off with a piece of wood; such is the process of shaving. After this performance we all got a ducking, and had various games, which chiefly consisted in competitions such as climbing ropes hand over hand, etc.

'We took a hundred and one days to go to Sydney, which is about the average passage, but we did not meet many ships or steamers on the way. Sydney is a very magnificent place. It has one of the finest harbours in the world, being over a thousand miles round from one head to another. The scenery, as one goes in, is beautiful, all kinds of trees, flowers and birds abound there which I have not seen before. When we dropped anchor the doctor came on board, we were all lined up and examined, bared our chests and showed our tongues to see if we were free from plague. Next, the police came to inquire whether there had been any little disturbances, but we had had none. After that, the ship was crowded with men selling fruit, and all kinds of food which we were all ready to buy, the fruit being quite a change from salt horse and pea soup. We had to lie in Mosmon's Bay three days before we could go alongside, remaining there over Sunday. The chaplain of Missions to Seamen came on board and brought us some books. Our Vicar (Rev. W. Wynne Jones) – who always had a good word to say for Jack – had very kindly given me a letter of introduction to the chaplain which helped me on very much. When we got ashore, where we were allowed to go at six, after knocking off work, I went to the 'Missions to Seamen's Hall'. There I met a crowd of fellows from other ships, there was plenty of amusement, and a concert was held nearly every night. I got to know some very nice people in Sydney and went to the theatre several times, and also visited the beautiful Botanical Gardens which cover an area of several miles. Unfortunately we were only there for seventeen days, so I was unable to see much, not being allowed ashore until six o'clock.

'As half our cargo was for Newcastle (which is sixty miles north of Sydney) we were towed there, arriving at Newcastle at five o'clock in the morning. This place is not to be compared with Sydney, but it is a large coal shipping port. There are two Mission Halls here but they do not come up to the one at Sydney. We were in Newcastle nine weeks loading coals for Caleta Coloso, S. America, where we arrived on Christmas Eve.

'This is a very small port which has only been opened about five years. There were many ships there waiting for cargoes. In the ports on the Chilian Coast the ships do not go alongside a wharf but lie at anchor, and barges come off, and we have to discharge freights, 'black diamonds', into them. The 'Old Man' (captain) goes ashore every morning and afternoon and the apprentices who row him ashore fish all the time during his stay there. The fish are so numerous that there is no occasion to use bait, one ties three hooks together, throws them out, and gives sudden long jerks; one often catches two or three at a time. Sea-lions abound there and come quite close to the boats. Several of the apprentices went out fishing with dynamite, and when it was let off hundreds of fish of all sizes came to the surface stunned, and we had a full boat load, which was salted down for future use. At night time we used to put a light over the side of the ship and the fish would come to the surface in numbers, then the sea-lions would come, which we used to harpoon, taking thirteen altogether, some being very large. Whenever they were hauled on deck we had to lasso them, to prevent their big teeth from doing damage. The quickest way to kill one of these animals is to give it a sharp tap on the 'snuffbone'. We used to keep the skin for making boots, and out of their flappers we made several tobacco pouches.

'We could not get a cargo of nitrate at this port for home, so had to load ballast for Talcahuano, a little south of Valparaiso. We took nearly a month, being very unlucky in that. We found it very cold there after being in the tropics so long. The day before we arrived in Talcahuano we had two whales around the ship for the whole day, and they would come and rub themselves against the ship's bottom to take the barnacles off their backs. Their blow-holes, from which they spout water, are large enough for a man to go down. The only objection one has to them is the disagreeable odour they cast off.

'Talcahuano is a Naval Port; there were a number of the Chilian Fleet there, which were constantly practising firing at targets in the bay. Fruit is very cheap out there, grapes being a penny a pound, apples and pears being as plentiful as peas. We loaded wheat at this port for Queenstown. Five other vessels were bound for this port, and we beat them all, making the second-best passage between the two ports for that week. We had a nasty time around the 'Horn' with snow squalls. We saw some icebergs, and the rigging was all covered with ice. We also experienced a very strong gale, disabling half the crew, the Mate being knocked down unconscious amongst them.

'Crossing the line we passed a dismasted barque, which had been in Talcahuano with us; we spoke to her through the megaphone and inquired of her if she were alright; she replied that she had had a bad time but could manage to get home if no more accidents happened. Next day we saw a shark swimming around the ship, and we baited a hook for it; about half an hour afterwards it hooked itself, and then it was played until it was exhausted; then we dropped a running bowline over its tail and it took five men to haul it aboard; it weighed over three hundredweight and measured twelve feet three inches; it had four rows of ugly-looking teeth on each jaw. When its stomach was ripped up, a tin, an old shoe, and a piece of rag were found there; its tail was cut off and nailed on the end of our jib-boom. This is always done on board a sailing vessel, as sailors, being very superstitious, say it frightens away the head winds. Two or three little fish, called Pilot Fish, precede every shark. They are very pretty, being striped like zebras; they guide the shark to wherever there is food to be found.

'We arrived at Queenstown eighty-eight days out. We

were all glad to arrive at a British Port, and worked with a will. After ten days' detention we received our orders for Antwerp, where we arrived ten days later. We came away without seeing much of the town, and arrived home in good health and spirits'.

This little document is interesting on more than one level. As pure narrative, it provides a lively picture of the ways in which young apprentices coped with the conditions of their strange and challenging new life, while its confident, matter-of-fact style reminds us that the writer belonged to the first generation of Welsh seamen to be educated on formal lines in a County School. Of at least equal interest is the character of the writer himself, who clearly emerges as a brisk and buoyant young man, temperamentally prepared to accept things as they come and well equipped to face life in all its vagaries.

Hugh Rees was the second son of Mr and Mrs John Rees, Glan Menai, North Road, Caernarfon, and a first cousin of the Misses Rees who lived in Plas Brereton from 1899 until the 1960s. It would be pleasant to record that he eventually fulfilled promise of his early apprenticeship on the *Gwydyr Castle* by becoming a Master Mariner of some distinction, but the fates decreed otherwise. According to two entries in the *Carnarvon & Denbigh Herald*, he completed his apprenticeship on the *Gwydyr*, succeeded in gaining his Second Mate's ticket, and was actually serving in that capacity 'on a ship' (un-named) when war broke out in August 1914. For reasons best known to himself but which are not too difficult to guess, he promptly resigned his post at sea to volunteer as a private in the Army, and it was not long before he was granted a commission in the 16th Battalion of the Royal Welch Fusiliers. Within less than two years, on the 16th July 1916, Lieutenant Hugh Tregarthen

Rees was killed in the action which led to the capture of Mametz Wood, and his name may be found among the many which cover the base of the Caernarfon Cenotaph. He was 24 years old.

The voyage which he described so blithely in *The Arvonian* ended in the Autumn of 1908. Shortly after Mother arrived in Nefyn, she gave birth to her second child, a boy called John Ifor.

* * *

January 1909 saw the start of their third trip from here to Australia, their first port of call this time being Melbourne. This gave Mother a chance to meet her brother-in-law John and his family at their home in 'Nevin Cottage' on the outskirts of that city. Father was familiar enough with the place, for, whenever his ship docked in Melbourne, there on the quayside was John to insist upon his coming out to 'Nevin' as soon as his duties allowed. Father therefore knew what a warm welcome awaited him there, and it was not long before Mother also experienced the same hospitality. Time and again I heard her say that, for them, 'Nevin' was a home from home.

On our way to Melbourne, however, we ran into trouble, when off Cape Leuwin we were struck by a particularly vicious gale. Neither Father nor anyone else on board had ever experienced anything like it, and Mother could well believe this as she listened to the wind screaming in the sheets and watched the seas cascading down upon them from a great height. The ship was quickly hove-to, and oil-bags were draped over the sides to counter the force of the gale. For a while such measures proved effective, and there was a lull during which the *Gwydyr* lay in comparative stillness like a leaf on a river in flood. But at sea one must always expect the unexpected, and it came this time in the shape of a gigantic wave which appeared from nowhere, striking the ship on her beam with such force that she came within an ace of capsizing. In Mother's words:

'Mercifully she did not heel right over, and the men at the wheel stood their ground like rocks and kept her resolutely on course. By the time that she had righted herself and was once more on an even keel, we found that 2 of her 4 boats were reduced to matchwood, and much more damage came to light later, but by some miracle no lives were lost and no one was seriously hurt... When we approached Melbourne, we passed a P. & O. Liner which had been caught in the same storm and had its upper bridge torn clean away by the gale'.

Once again, after repairs had been completed, we went through the familiar routine of plying across the Pacific between the main Australian ports and the coasts of Chile and Peru. An incident during one of these passages is recorded in a snapshot dated the 25th May 1910. It shows my sister and myself with an albatross which has landed on the deck and been captured by the men. As every schoolboy knows, the albatross is graceful in flight but clumsy and helpless on the ground – a fact borne out by this snapshot which makes the bird look like a taxidermist's model when in reality it is alive. My sister leans against it, whilst I sit side-saddle on its back. Perhaps the fact that I was only 19 months old explains why this picture rings no bells in my mind.

Mother found more exciting ways of enjoying herself. Once, while the ship was discharging in Callao, she had what she described as 'an unforgettable experience'. The local agent invited her and Father to visit some coppermines in the hinterland of Lima, in the high mountain country of Cerro de Pasco in the Andes. They travelled by truck on a narrow railway, taking over 2 hours for the journey uphill and less than 20 minutes on the way down. Whenever Mother was asked to recount the details – the open truck, the steep incline, the breakneck speed at which they whirled round the bends, with towering cliffs on one hand and a precipitous drop on the other – she wondered how on earth she could have survived, let alone enjoy it. But enjoy it she did.

According to one old postcard, it was in Tocopilla that I had my second birthday and was initiated into the mysteries of kicking a ball on dry land. My tutor was our West Indian steward, who was addressed by everyone else as Mr Charles but whom for some reason I knew as Tom-tom.

Perhaps I should explain that I spent my short life at sea under the wing of two special guardians. One was an enormous Irish wolfhound called Tiger who began his life in Nefyn as member of the family of Dr Hughes 'Y Dderwen' but who early on in his career had a brush with the law when he succumbed to the urge to hunt and harry sheep. The local farmers were understandably out for his blood and it came as no surprise to anyone when the Doctor was officialy told to put him down. Not having the heart to kill such a magnificent animal, he pleaded with Father to take the dog away to sea, where it would be safe from both the temptations of the chase and the long arm of the law. Father readily agreed, and Tiger joined our family as to the manner born. He could be fierce enough towards strangers and some members of the crew, but in his handling of children he was gentleness itself. When I was small enough to stay in my cradle, he would lie by my side and snarl menacingly at all who ventured too close. Later, when I became mobile, he would cling to me like a shadow, always on the seaward side.

My other guardian was Tom-tom. As time went by and I began to distinguish between humans and dogs, he gradually took over from Tiger as my inseparable companion. It was he who taught me that there were such things as games. Once at least he saved my life, when I leaned too far over the edge of the open hold and he grabbed me by the ankle as I prepared to dive head first into the depths. Mother, standing by the saloon door, was a petrified witness of this incident.

After leaving Tocopilla a few weeks before Christmas, we came home round the Horn, and one episode in that passage impressed itself so clearly on my mind that I can still recall it in detail. One day, as I came out of the cabin, I saw wisps of fog swirling across the ship. From time to time a booming sound came from beyond the rails, and men moved rapidly here and there. All these details, vivid though they were, would have meant little to me if I had not described them to Mother many years later so that she could explain them to me. The booming sound, she told me, was caused by icebergs floating up from the South Pole and, as they drifted into warmer waters, splitting apart with a crack like thunder. We were in a field of these bergs when the fog closed in to make confusion worse confounded. This did not help the Second Mate, who lost his head, started yelling "Ddown ni byth o'r fan'ma'n fyw',[8] and had to be kept under lock and key until the emergency was over. According to Mother, 'There is no doubt that we owed our lives to your father's coolness and seamanship'. She never told me the name of the unfortunate Second Mate, and it was not until some 12 years ago that, quite by accident, I discovered his identity. He was not from Nefyn.

---

[8] 'We will never come out of this place alive'.

5

Gwydyr Castle: Voyage 4

The final series of family voyages began in the early summer of 1911. It was from other people, naturally, that I learned the details of this, as of the previous voyage, together with the names of the places which we visited, but by 1911 I was becoming old enough to be able to commit to memory some at least of the things which happened to me.

I remember that the name of our First Mate was Mr Leighton, an English gentleman and a fine seaman, and that the Second Mate was a friendly character from Borthygest called Griff Roberts. Since those days Captain Griffith Roberts O.B.E., has more than once told me that he and Mr Leighton made a point of watching me like two hawks and that, if they suspected that I was likely to be 'up to no good', they would hold me over the rail in the fore-peak and threaten to drop me overboard unless I promised to behave myself. What a modern psychologist would make of such treatment is a good question, but, according to Captain Griff Roberts, it always produced the desired result. So far as I am aware, it left no painful scars on my mind.

After reaching Sydney and discharging our cargo, we moved on to Hobart, where the goods taken aboard included a number of birds and animals destined for Lima Zoo. At one stage the deck was covered with cages of various sizes, each one occupied either by some unfamiliar beast or by a colourful assortment of parrots and cockatoos. One of the animals which first riveted my attention was a ferocious bear-like creature, about the size of a large domestic cat, which arched its back and spat venomously whenever anyone drew near. This, I was told, was a Tasmanian Devil.

Its uncompromising hostility and the villainous look in its eyes gradually wore me down and I transferred my interest to a pair of wallabies who proved far more amiable and even allowed me to step inside their quarters. I shall never forget the thrill of approaching their cage one morning and finding that the family of two had increased overnight to three. It was the first miracle that I ever saw with my own eyes.

In Callao the first person to welcome us was Captain Roberts of the *Ravenhill* which was berthed a short distance away. We spent much time in his company during the next few weeks, as we waited for the *Gwydyr* to be re-loaded for a trip back to Sydney. Since there was little to do in Callao itself and Lima was only about 8 miles away, we frequently went there by train to while away the warm and sunny afternoons.

One of the most attractive spots in Lima was a large park where tall trees threw cool shadows over the lawns and flowerbeds, and where we could sit on comfortable benches to listen to a military band playing in a small pagoda. The band's mascot was a large hairy sheep-like animal. Captain Roberts told me that it was a llama and that I should be well advised to leave it alone. Later, when I was tired of trotting along the paths and across the turf, I forgot the captain's advice, went over to the llama and began to stroke its neck. It responded by biting a huge semi-circle out of the panama hat which I was wearing. I therefore ran back to my parents to deposit what was left of my hat, but, when I returned to the animal and resumed my overtures, it proceeded to make a hearty meal of my hair, at which point I called off the engagement.

Captain Roberts and I received a warmer welcome when he took me to the zoo to see my old shipmates the wallabies. They were then housed in much roomier premises than on the deck of the *Gwydyr*, but they remained as friendly as ever, and, long before we had reached the bars of their enclosure, they rushed towards us and began to hop and gibber with excitement. Lifted on Captain Roberts's arms, I was even allowed to stroke their heads.

On the 12th December 1911 we left Callao for Sydney, and for the early part of the trip we had favourable winds and generally fine weather. Seventeen days out, on the 29th December, we approached Pitcairn Island and came close enough inshore for some of the islanders to come out in their longboats to row alongside, to exchange news, and to wish us well. A few were also interested in a possible bargain. These men were of course the descendants of the sailors who mutinied on *HMS Bounty* and started a new life on Pitcairn. Among the items which Mother bought from them was a book giving a detailed account of the events which followed the mutiny, and the Mr William McCoy from whom she bought it claimed to be a grandson of one of the original mutineers.

Beyond Pitcairn the weather worsened and within two or three days there were clear signs that we must be on the fringes of a cyclone. As Mother described it: 'The first signs came when the glass began to fall, slowly at first, then more sharply as we moved ahead. When the wind struck, the swell which had been running with increasing momentum became a succession of high waves streaked with foam and filling the air with spray. The sky was full of dense black clouds, torrential rain joined the spray and was driven almost horizontally by gusts of shrieking wind, while flashes were to be seen somewhere in the distance. Fortunately, we suffered no serious damage, although one heavy sea did strike the ship a glancing blow which threatened to send her spinning out of control.' Despite the noise and the excitement, I have no recollection of this storm. Perhaps I was asleep.

What I do remember with perfect clarity is standing by the rail in the forepeak one day, watching a group of men in bare feet throwing fishing lines over the side. Suddenly one of them hauled in his line and drew on board a large, long fish with a number of tiny fish clinging to its sides. He picked up one of the tiny fish, told me to watch him, and then carefully placed it on his instep. When, a few seconds later, he brushed it away, his instep was bleeding. This was one of the many occasions when the apprentices amused themselves during the quieter spells in the Doldrums by catching sharks so that they could use the flesh as bait for more edible fish.

After discharging in Sydney, we sailed in ballast to Melbourne, where we received the statutory welcome from Uncle John and his family. Many happy hours were spent playing in their house and garden. Nevertheless, Melbourne is a place which I recall with mixed feelings. For one thing, it was there that I contracted a bout of measles, the first symptoms of which made themselves felt as I was riding on the back of an elephant in the Zoo. It was there also that I fell on the deck, cut open my forehead on an iron ring-bolt, and precipitated a minor crisis. After Father had applied first-aid to stem the bleeding, he ran ashore to find a doctor, whom he doggedly traced to a chemist's shop and who had to be almost literally frog-marched back to the ship, for the poor man had been looking forward to an evening's fishing. When he had sterilised and stitched the wound, he expressed the view that, if my sister had lost as much blood, she would probably not be alive, and that it was only thanks to the grace of a strong constitution that I was still around . . . In due course my period of convalescence was over and I was allowed to run loose again, only to stumble in the self-same spot, hit the same ring-bolt, and re-open the gash.

It was while we were in Melbourne that Mother

discovered for certain that her third child was on the way. She was anxious that it should be born in Britain, and, since the *Gwydyr* was scheduled to make yet another trip to Chile, it was decided that Mother, my sister, and I should come home by steam. We were lucky enough to be able to book a passage on the White Star liner *Persic*, of which Evan Davies (Nefyn) was Chief Officer.

On her way to Liverpool the *Persic* called in Hobart, Sydney, Durban, and Cape Town, and so provided us with our first, and last, chance to visit South Africa. One picture taken in Durban shows a stalwart Zulu wearing a magnificent head-dress of cow-horns and ostrich-plumes, and holding the shafts of a rickshaw with four passengers – Mother, another lady whom Mother may have met on board, my sister, and myself. Another picture taken about the same time shows, in the foreground, two greasy-pole competitors on the *Persic* watched by groups of spectators in the background, and was presumably taken when we celebrated the crossing of the Line with the traditional fun and games. I not only enjoyed the sports which were organised at that time but recall distinctly that I viewed most of them in the company of an elderly gentleman, a Scottish Presbyterian minister who was on his way home from New Zealand and with whom I spent much of my leisure time.

In Liverpool we had one whole day in which to recover our land legs, and then travelled on to Nefyn, where, in July 1912, my brother Gwilym Hugh was born. As our sister had now passed the age of 5 and was therefore legally compelled to attend school, our nomadic family life came to an abrupt end and we embarked upon a completely new chapter in our history.

6

Dry Land

As one might expect, Mother's feelings at the thought of having to turn her back on the sea were by no means unmixed. Despite her rough baptism, she had enjoyed the constant to-ing and fro-ing, and the unique opportunity not only to meet new friends in strange parts of the world but also to visit cities and continents which would otherwise have been known to her only from the pages of books and atlases.

Of the cities which she came to know well, she had a soft spot for Lima. She loved to refer to the beauty of its buildings, especially the cathedral, the flower gardens in the streets, and the natural courtesy of its inhabitants. She never cared much for Sydney; she found the bay beautiful beyond words, but the town itself shapeless and strident. Far more congenial was Melbourne, with its trees and its formal, rather staid symmetry . . . But, whatever the differences between those various places, they all had some special quality which made a deep impression upon her and filled her mind with memories which were to be a source of delight and enrichment to her for the rest of her life.

On the one hand, therefore, she faced with some misgiving the prospect of abandoning for ever a way of life which had brought such colour and variety into her life. On the other hand, she could not deny that life at sea, for her, had changed its character dramatically during the 7 years from 1905 to 1912, and that this change had not been for the better.

The main reason for the change was that my sister and I,

as soon as we became mobile, had begun to create problems which she had not altogether forseen. In our innocence we saw nothing wrong in doing things which might be tolerable on dry land but which, in the confined area of a ship at sea, were unacceptably anti-social – such things as pushing used match-sticks through the vents of the fresh-water tanks, taking out the putty which the men had laboriously placed between the planks on deck, or any one of the innumerable misdeeds which kept Mr Leighton and Griff Roberts so purposefully on their toes.

One Sunday afternoon in Callao, while everybody else enjoyed a much-needed siesta, my sister found a pot of paint and a brush left behind the door of the lazaret, and took it into her head to decorate every part of the saloon which she could reach, including chairs and table-legs, cushions, doors, and carpet. My father apparently took such antics philosophically and was even privately amused by some of them, but Mother could not afford to be so detached, and heaven knows what a strain they placed upon her patience. Even worse was the fact that restless children faced constant dangers in such a confined space. The most dangerous thing that we could do was to clamber on to the poop where only a rail stood between us and the water. With a swell running, the risks were magnified. All in all, it was a life with literally no dull moments. I still have some tiny scars to prove it. Mother's scars did not show, but she must have felt more than once that a ship like the *Gwydyr* was hardly the ideal place to bring up a family.

She also knew that life in Nefyn, however prosaic in comparison, would have its compensations. For the past 7 years it had been the home of her parents and their family; there too were many of her personal friends and most of Father's relations. In addition, Father and his brother-in-law John Williams had decided to invest their life-savings in 2 houses – Craigymôr and Minymôr – to be built in a field on the Morfa road almost directly opposite the school. The work on them had already begun and was expected to be completed by the summer or early autumn of 1913. It so happened, therefore, that Mother arrived home in time to be able to keep an eye on the closing stages of the building, so as to ensure that everything would be done in accordance with Father's wishes. Such a duty, added to the responsibility of rearing 3 children, would give her little time for regrets.

On a lower scale, my sister and I also had our problems, for in many respects our little world had been turned upside down. The first and most painful change was coming to terms with the fact that Father was no longer a constant member of the family. From being with us from day to day, he was suddenly transformed into a comparative stranger whom we were allowed to see only incidentally. It was gradually that we came to realise the full implications of the change which had taken place, but, ever since the moment when we had waved goodbye to him on the wharf in Melbourne as we steamed away on the *Persic*, we were nagged by the uneasy feeling that in some sense we had lost him, and arriving home in Nefyn without him was not a happy experience.

The fact that our experience was reflected in so many Nefyn families at that time might suggest that the social unit in which we grew up was lop-sided, incomplete, and inevitably dominated by women. Nothing could be further from the truth. At no time was there a noticeable shortage of men about the place, partly because there were several other men following the usual variety of occupations on dry land, not to mention many retired people, both native and immigrant, who had settled in the area. In addition, there was a solid core of quarrymen who, before the first World

War led to the closure of the Gwylwyr Quarry, formed a substantial part of the population. One of the latter group was Taid. The presence of such men ensured (among other things) that we were spared the worst excesses of petticoat government; for, whenever we needed male help or advice, there was usually a male relative on hand to give it. My own special mentor was Taid, and I grew to confide in him more and more as the months went by. At one stage, people who were not familiar with my name had a habit of referring to me as 'yr hogyn bach 'na sy'n perthyn i John Owen y Gwylwyr'.[9] Despite such substitutes, we missed Father and secretly envied those children whose fathers were always at home.

It was therefore a good thing that my sister had a school to go to and that I had more than enough to occupy my mind. Before I had made the startling discovery that there were other small boys to play with, one of my main distractions was the new house, where the final stages of building and decorating were, for me, a unique experience. I was not too young to realise that something unusual was in the wind, for Mother was so busy all day long that I found myself free to spend long hours exploring the site of the new garden, chasing such bizzare creatures as field-mice, lizards, grasshoppers, butterflies, small green frogs, hedgehogs, and other miracles. Once I met a weasel sliding out of the flower-border, but failed to catch it. On hot days the sky was never without a lark, and as the shadows lengthened the surrounding fields filled with rasping corncrakes. At the end of each day I would fill my pockets with bright caterpillars and similar treasures, and, after I had gone to bed, Mother never quite knew what creepy horror lay waiting for her when she came to my room to check that all was well.

The house itself was equally enthralling. Outside, bearded men in overalls painted the woodwork or flung pebble-dash at the walls; inside, there were large rooms full of echoes and the sweet smell of timber. In the bare, dusty kitchen, Mother was usually to be found either pouring tea or slicing a fresh loaf. My interest in all these proceedings was shared by a large green parrot, a friendly character whose vocabulary grew steadily over the next few years and eventually embraced snatches of 'Tipperary' and other contemporary classics.

Another distraction was Canton House, a grocer's shop just down the road on the lower side of the well. The owner, Mr Hugh Jones, was a deacon in Capel Soar and a local preacher of some repute whose unquestioned talent for textual criticism was fatally undermined by his failure to come to terms with his dentures. He had a son, Davy Richard, whose main job it was to deliver orders in a trap drawn by a sturdy brown pony. As a rule, his duties took him to Pistyll or up the mountain, but once in a while he would drive to the old warehouses on the beach of Portinllaen to collect sacks of flour and other merchandise brought by sea from Liverpool or Runcorn for the farmers and shopkeepers of Lleyn. My joy was complete whenever he took me with him, although he once alarmed me by walking the pony into the sea and casually announcing his intention to float the trap across the bay. Being accustomed to stauncher craft, I allowed my alarm to show, whereupon, with an ostentatious show of reluctance, he turned back towards the shore and completed the journey on land. On reflection, I felt ashamed and determined to make amends for such a deplorable lack of spirit. Therefore, on every subsequent visit to Portinllaen, I pleaded with him to take to the water, only to be rebuffed rather superciliously, and reminded that life is not in the habit of offering a second chance.

If I happened to be at Canton House in the evening when the pony was released from the shafts, I was lifted on to its back and we were then led past the side of the shop to a small, snug stable lit by a dim lantern and filled with the warm scent of hay. Either the pony was fat or else my legs were short, for, as we made the sharp left-hand bend towards the stable door, the toe of my right foot always scraped against the whitewashed wall at precisely the same spot, leaving a mark which lasted for years. It was a splendid way to end the day and served as an extra reminder that, despite the great disparity in our ages, Davy Richard in those days was my closest friend.

Almost as splendid were those days when Taid took me with him to the quarry, where the narrow railway ran down the steep hillside and across the main road before coming to rest on the pier, which jutted out for about 100 yards into the sea. If we followed the path across the hill from Llwynffynnon, we passed through a wonderland of gorse and bracken and tall grass where anything might happen. Rabbits scampered across our path, birds flitted noisily from bush to bush, while the gorse-blossom fairly throbbed with the humming of the bees. Once we saw a badger being threatened, from a safe distance, by a barking sheep-dog from the nearby farm of Wern. Since the badger stood stock-still and the dog clearly had no intention of advancing any further, the whole operation appeared rather pointless, but it was a pretty sight.

The quarry itself also had its mysteries, as I realised one day when Taid took me there at a time when there seemed to be no one at work. While we were sauntering casually along a deserted gallery, we heard a shout which made us both look upwards, and there, on the skyline, appeared the figure of a man. He again shouted something which was gibberish to me but which prompted Taid to behave in a peculiar fashion. Approaching the rock face, he carefully placed me on a board shelf which had a roof to it, and hopped in beside me. He told me that we were about to hear a loud bang. And there we lay, in a state of suspended animation, until the bang came, followed almost immediately by the noise of falling debris as boulders of various shapes and sizes flew or slid past our hiding-place. Soon there was silence. When Taid was satisfied that the silence had come to stay, he hopped out of the shelter, placed me once more upon the ground, and explained what had happened. The incident left me rather breathless and bewildered, but everything had happened so quickly that there was literally no time to feel afraid.

Once in a blue moon we might venture further afield. There was one long summer's day when Mother and Nain hired a pony and trap from Mr Robert Roberts 'Y Wern' and took me along to visit some friends in Trefor. We travelled via Llithfaen, leaving Nefyn after an early breakfast and returning late in the evening. On the homeward leg, the sun was gradually blotted out and we ran into a torrential thunderstorm, with rain like stair-rods, and lurid flashes which lit up the hills and the whole of Caernarfon Bay. It was a beautiful and eerie display, but I was more impressed by the fact that the pony appeared totally unconcerned and that Nain's umbrella kept us all dry.

---

[9] 'That little boy related to John Owen y Gwylwyr'.

7

Finding one's bearings

One of the odd features of becoming a landlubber was having to adjust oneself to an ever-growing circle of friends and acquaintances. Whenever I happened to be out of doors, total strangers whom I had never met before were likely to address me by my name. Evidently they knew me and presumably expected me to know them. This was disconcerting.

So was the unholy tangle of relationships on both sides of the family. Small boys as a rule are so concerned with the visible and tangible things around them that they have little time to occupy themselves with the niceties of personal connections, either within or outside the family, and I was no exception to that rule.

Luckily for me, my mother's parents, John and Miriam Owen, presented no serious problem, for they lived within a few hundred yards of our home and I saw them literally every day. Nain was small, slight, and dark, with the gentlest smile and the sweetest disposition imaginable, although she also had a firm hand and a will of her own. Taid, on the other hand, was a big man with sandy hair, a luxuriant moustache of the same colour, blue eyes, and the reputation of being one of the best quarrymen in the area. He was also a rigorous disciplinarian. Sharing their home at Brynhyfryd were their 3 youngest children, Myfanwy, Enid and Idris. Of the others, Naomi had married Charles Baum of Trefor and emigrated to Wisconsin, Phoebe (with a degree in Classics) was teaching in Trefor, Miriam worked as a clerk in the Gwylwyr Quarry Office, and John Richard had joined the staff of the Ministry of Pensions in Cardiff.

On my father's side, the spectrum of relationships was much more confusing. Both his parents had died at an early age, and his brother John was a long way off in Australia, but he also had two married sisters who lived within easy reach of us and of each other. Auntie Jane and her son Jack were our nextdoor neighbours, while Auntie Annie and her husband John Griffith were only a few yards down the road in a house called 'Gwenallt'.

Much further afield, outside the limits of the village, were a number of father's cousins. Three of them, John and Dai Davies and Annie Ellis, lived with their mother (Auntie Mary) in my grandmother's old home Penrallt. This was a delightful spot which we normally approached from the back, along a long narrow field which led to a small duck-pond where squadrons of poultry swam or splashed around, while other quacked or clucked their way across the yard under the watchful eye of two farm cats. On one side of the yard, opposite the back of the house, were out-houses for storing hay and other fodder, and a shed for 3 or 4 cows.

At the front of the house were trees which produced the most succulent apples ever known to man. At certain seasons of the year, when Mother forbade us to pick fruit, we were reduced to nibbling pieces off them as they hung upon the branches; but later in the year a gentle shake of the tree was enough to convert them into legitimate windfalls.

I have only a blurred recollection of Auntie Mary as a small, brown figure constantly bustling about the kitchen or the buttery, but her 3 children survived into the 1930s. Both the sons wore beards, but, whereas John was tall and fair like a Viking, Dai was square and dark, with a look which suggested that he had a saturnine side to his nature.

It was not often that we saw Uncle John of Penrallt, as he was captain of the White Star liner *Cedric* and spent most of his time in Liverpool. Uncle Dai too had gone to sea as a boy, but had a tragic experience which effectively blighted his career. He was on the bridge entering New York harbour in thick fog when his ship rammed a tug and split it in two, leaving no survivors. For the rest of his life he suffered violent epileptic attacks which made a career at sea unthinkable. The saturnine side of his nature showed itself whenever we met, for his idea of a joke was to shake us by the hand and then squeeze it until we jumped; but he always stopped short of hurting us, and the first thing that he did after letting us go was to poke his fingers inside his left waistcoat pocket and give us a 'mint imperial' which smelled faintly of tobacco.

Uncle Dai's constant companion was a large yellow sheepdog called King, the most venomous animal that I have ever had to face outside a cage. King was well aware of his master's ailment, and, when one of the latter's fits occurred, the dog would act like a demented dervish, rushing wildly about the yard, howling desperately, and hurling itself sideways against the farmhouse door.

Auntie Annie (Ellis) was a widow, but, although she invariably wore black, her manner was bright and friendly. It was rumoured that, when the occasion demanded strong measures, she had a sharp and even shrewish tongue, but we never heard it at work. On the contrary, she was always so glad to see us and her welcome was so ingenuously cordial that we jumped at every opportunity to visit Penrallt to collect butter and eggs or a pailful of buttermilk, despite the fact that the dreaded King would canter to meet us at the boundary stile and escort us to the house, barking or snarling at us all the way. We found that stage of the journey a terrifying experience, and the sheer effort of trying to keep our nerves under control left us limp and exhausted, but Auntie Annie's reception more than made up for the discomfort, and a glass of fresh buttermilk never failed to restore our spirits ... She always had two cats, one of which was called Miss Andrews after a family friend, and the other Lloyd George. Whenever she gave us a kitten to keep the field-mice away from Craigymôr, it was on the clear understanding that it be given one of those two names. Sometimes the kitten had been formally christened before we received it.

Three fields away from Penrallt, on the Morfa side, was Pwll William, a similar farmhouse surrounded by tall privet hedges and bright fuchsia bushes, and facing the pond which gave it its name. This pond was a source of great joy to us in our young days. It was there that I saw my first heron standing erect on one leg in the shallows and looking as though it had no other function than to be quaintly decorative ... There in the summer we watched the waterhens paddling sedately from one patch of weeds to the next, with their convoy of chicks in line astern ... In winter, during the cold snaps, the pond could turn overnight into a skating rink where we were free to slither about with careless and artless abandon until our bodies were black and blue.

The farmhouse was the home of my grandmother's second sister, Modryb Ann. Whenever we called to see her, she was always to be found in the same place, huddled in a corner of the front parlour on the right-hand side of the fireplace, clothed in black from top to toe, a small lace cap perched on her head and a lace shawl draped across her shoulders. The window behind her lit up a room that was chockful of brass and china ornaments. She cannot have been much older than 60 when I first saw her, but her stillness made her seem ageless. She also seemed remote and mysterious, for she was totally blind. And although she always greeted us kindly, we had the uncomfortable feeling that she lived in a timeless world of her own.

Of her 3 children, Uncle John was away at sea, had found a wife in Nefyn and established his new home there; Auntie Ann was married to a sailor called John Wmffras but continued to live at Pwll William during her husband's voyages; Auntie Mary was a plump, brown spinstress who had decided that in no circumstances would she leave her mother... It was with Auntie Mary that we usually had fun. If she happened to be milking when we crossed the yard, she would tell us to open our mouths wide so that she could direct a stream of milk straight between our lips... However heartily we might relish such games, the intricate pattern of Mary's and Ann's and John's made life confusing for at least one small boy.

Six more of my father's cousins lived just across the water in Holyhead. They were there because the third of my grandmother's sisters had gone to Porthmadog to work as a young girl, married a certain John Williams who was employed as a carpenter in the local shipyards, and in time moved with him to Holyhead, where he found a job with the mail-boat company. Their eventual family consisted of 5 daughters and one son. The son, Evan, not surprisingly went to sea. He was one of my father's closest friends and acted as his best man in 1905, although he himself remained throughout his life the staunchest of bachelors. When I knew him, he was a burly jovial captain on the Holyhead-Kingstown mail-boats, with the enviable reputation of being a first-class seaman who never missed a tide because he could sniff his way across in the thickest fog.

8

Two Years of Peace

After my brother's birth in 1912 we enjoyed 2 years of peace before the Great War began. During that interlude Father was persuaded, for wholly pecuniary reasons, to leave the *Gwydyr Castle* and take command of the *Belford*, a full-rigged ship of some 1,900 tons, built in 1894 and belonging to the same company as the *Gwydyr*.

It is sad to reflect that we never saw the *Gwydyr* again. She was destined to be sold after the war to Job Brothers of New Brunswick, who later re-sold her to Rajcoomer of Port Louis, Mauritius. According to an entry in *Sea Breezes*, she did the run from Fremantle to Port Louis in 24 days shortly before she was laid up. It was probably in 1928 that this happened, and her name appears for the last time in Lloyd's Register for 1935-36.

The single most important thing that happened to me as an individual was that I was compelled to join the Infants' Department of the local school, where the teacher in charge was Miss Ellis, a conscientious lady with a kind heart but a nervous manner, who was often harassed into treating us far more harshly than she perhaps intended. During the two years which we spent under her protective wing, she clucked over us like an over-anxious hen which sees a fox behind every bush, and pecked us smartly if we so much as threatened to wander out of range.

Her brood was so large that she could not afford to show much discrimination, but there can be no doubt that she took a serious view of her role 'in loco parentis'. Only once did I dare to play truant, with Robin 'Penbryn' and Robin 'Bull', and on that occasion the fact that poor Miss Ellis had bad feet which made ordinary walking painful did not prevent her from running down Lôn Gam until she spotted us, and then chasing us all the way across the sands to Creigiau Bach until we realised that (since she had obviously recognised us and had no intention of giving up the chase) discretion was the better part of valour, and we might as well throw ourselves upon her mercy.

Many years later, long after she had retired from teaching and become the wife of Mr John Ellis Jones the village postmaster, she continued to take a lively and talkative interest in our progress, such as it was. We duly discovered that she was in her way a diplomat, for during the Second World War, whenever she greeted former pupils who happened to be home on leave, or whenever she made enquiries about those who were abroad, she was likely to confer upon them a higher rank than they were strictly entitled to. My brother, who was away for some years in North Africa and Italy, was rapidly promoted in his absence to the rank of Major.

It was under her spirited guidance that, from 1913-15, I had my first taste of formal instruction and was unceremoniously hustled into the paths of Rectitude and of the other three Rs. My progress in these disciplines was twice interrupted by injury, for the mixed fortunes which I had experienced at sea followed me ashore, and within a few months I had broken both legs.

The first accident happened in Canton House on a day when the floor had been lightly sprinkled with water and become so slippery that, rushing into the shop, I inadvertently did the splits and found it impossible to pick myself up without support. After a good deal of anxious prodding, the other people in the shop decided that home was the best place for me. Some hours elapsed before Dr Griffith arrived and placed me on my back on the kitchen table so that he could find out what was wrong and then pull the limb back into place. Never before or since have I perspired as much as I did during that brief operation.

The second accident occurred one lunch-time on a building site near the school, where the Doctor, then living in Rhianfa, had commissioned a new house which was to be called Egryn. It was made clear to us in school that on no account were we to set foot on this building site – an edict more honoured in the breach than in th'observance. When I fell off the scaffolding, my good leg snapped at the knee, but my fellow-trespassers half-carried me to school, where I spent the afternoon in painful attempts to conceal the fact that we had been out of bounds. So long as I remained inert, the pain was tolerable, but whenever I was ordered to move briskly 'up the bench' and the teacher pushed me because my rate of progress was too slow, my hair stood on end. No one guessed what was wrong. By the end of the day, when it was plain to everybody that I could hardly move and that one of my legs was fractionally shorter than the other, they placed me on the classroom table and sent for my mother. She wheeled me in my brother's pushchair to Rhianfa, where Dr Griffith made blustery noises befoe once more yanking me back to normal. Then I was tenderly carried home to enjoy another period of convalescence.

As my bed overlooked Well Street with its steady trickle of carts and people, my inactivity was not hard to bear. I even discovered that being a semi-invalid for a limited period can have built-in advantages. Friends of all ages showed their sympathy by being generous with their time and gifts, and when, on one and the same day, Mr Roberts brought a clutch of ducks' eggs all the way from Y Wern, and Father sent a rocking-horse in a wooden crate all the way from Liverpool, I learned the truth of what Harold Nicolson was to discover many years later, that 'one of the minor pleasures of life is to be slightly unwell'.

It was soon after my recovery that we went to live in the new Craigymôr, where it took us some time to find our bearings. We were now much closer to the school but correspondingly further from the shops, and Mother took the view that, if I was old enough to attend school, I was responsible enough to undertake a few errands now and again. In general, this was an unwelcome chore, as it often clashed with more urgent plans, but there were at least 4 places which had uncommon delights to offer.

One was the druggist's shop which we entered by climbing a short but steep flight of steps before opening a narrow door which announced our arrival by setting off a loud, insistent bell. The usual purpose of our visit was to buy some 'squills a paragoric', a cough cure which combined infallibility with a pleasant taste. As we waited for this nostrum to be dispensed behind the scenes, we vainly tried to identify the various smells which filled the air, while our eyes were bemused by the marvels surrounding us – tall cabinets glittering with coloured glass and exotic articles of all kinds, serried ranks of bottles with cryptic labels and signs, and, above all, enormous onion-shaped beakers filled with blue, green, or crimson liquid, tantalisingly just out of reach as they blinked in the sunlight. The owner of this Aladdin's Cave was Mr Williams, a frail, elderly man with a patrician manner, a wispy white beard, and a slender frame. He was so lame that, although he managed to hobble unaided about his premises, he never ventured outside without a pair of crutches. We were therefore amazed to find that he was a keen swimmer, and on the beach during the summer months we often watched him swing along into the water until it was deep enough for him to float and strike out in a steady breast-stroke, leaving his crutches to drift on the surface until he returned.

Immediately opposite the druggist's shop was a grocery store, Siop Glanrafon, owned by Mr and Mrs Roberts whose 3 daughters were married, respectively, to Captain Lloyd 'Moorings', Captain Jones 'Cynlas', and Captain Rowlands. Both Mrs Lloyd and Mrs Jones had left home, but Mrs Rowlands continued to help her parents in the shop, and, if sugar or tea happened to figure on my shopping-list, it was a revelation to watch her place a dark blue sheet of paper on the counter and, without any apparent effort, convert it into an elegant container for the required merchandise. The simple speed and precision of her movements raised the operation to the level of fine art, and ever since those days it has been my ambition (still unrealised) to pack a parcel with comparable skill . . . Equally deft was the way in which she would pick up a shapeless slab of butter and, with a series of casual and graceful flourishes, mould it into a perfectly symmetrical form.

A short distance away, in Stryd Plas was a shoe-repairer's shop where further sleight of hand was provided by Mr Ensor and his son George. They stood working at a high window overlooking the street, with their mouths full of tiny nails which they somehow flung with lightning rapidity on to a piece of leather before ramming them home with a hammer. It was no surprise to learn that they were popularly referred to as 'cryddion buan'.[10]

The fourth place which had something special to offer was Siop Alun House at the bottom of Well Street, or, more precisely, the Alun House bakery which stood just around the corner from the shop in the narrow Wint. Both shop and bakery belonged to Mr Thomas Williams, a tall man with fine dark moustaches and a white apron, who strode purposefully from one part of his domain to the other. It was he who baked Mother's bread, and, when the time came to collect it, he would open the wide oven door, push into its vast depths a flat ladle with a handle as long as a bargepole, and, despite the intense heat which made me cower against the wall, unerringly extract the correct tin with its fragrant loaf inside.

Carrying the bread home through Lleiniau and past Caeau Capel was a stern test of character, for the smell was irresistible, and the crust so crisp and so easily detachable that any boy with a palate was reduced to praying for strength to reach home before it had all gone. Not always were those prayers answered.

---

[10] The phrase describes the speed with which they worked.

9

The 1914-18 War

The 1914 War, although it affected our lives in many ways, was at first too remote and impersonal to make any real impact on the children of my age. In its early stages especially it bore less relationship to life as we knew it than to tales of derring-do which we had heard at home or in school. I remember hearing the word 'khaki' for the first time, and Mother explaining to us why that colour was preferable to red in modern war. It was the first hint of realism.

My clearest memory of August 1914 is of an afternoon spent with Nain at Glyn-y-Weddw, that attractive little mansion which still stands by the water's edge at Llanbedrog. We went by bus to Pwllheli, where Nain bought me a soldier's cap which had previously caught my eye in the window of Siop Goch and which remained fixed to my head for the rest of the day. We then caught the horse-drawn tram for Llanbedrog. The tramline started near the Post Office at the town end of Cardiff Road and continued as far as the West End before turning sharply to the right to complete the 3-mile trek across the sand-dunes. It was a beautiful day, and I can still re-live the pleasure of sitting there in the open tram, with the limitless sea on our left, listening to the scornful cries of the gulls, the squeak of leather and metal, and the steady thud of the pony's hooves upon the sand.

Glyn-y-Weddw in those days was an unusual combination of tea-rooms and art gallery, and for those who preferred to stay out of doors the grounds afforded a majestic view of Cardigan Bay . . . On our return to Pwllheli we had some time to wait for the Nefyn bus, and, as we strolled through the streets, we soon came within view of Salem chapel. The small square in front of the chapel was full of people, listening intently to a tall man in khaki uniform who stood on a platform of sorts. Nain seemed to be interested in what he had to say. Many years later she explained to me that the tall man was the Rev. John Williams, Brynsiencyn, presumably launching one of those recruiting drives which were to produce such a divided reaction in the Nonconformist conscience. That was the only time that I ever saw or heard that celebrated figure.

On rare occasions men in uniform might be seen walking through the streets of Nefyn. One afternoon my young brother and I joined a crowd by Old Post to watch a company of kilted troops, complete with drums, fifes, and bagpipes, drilling crisply on the Groes, and at one stage the Sergeant Major petrified me by asking my permission to pick up my brother and carry him down the line. This, too, it appears, was part of a recruiting campaign. Shortly afterwards there were rumours that most of the men had been killed in France . . . On another afternoon a destroyer steamed quietly into Nefyn Bay and spent a few hours there. Some of us were so enthralled by this strange apparition that the time slipped by un-noticed, and we had to run like fury in order to reach school just before it closed for the day, only to be spanked for our pains . . . But such episodes could only excite, without in any true sense affecting us, and it was only gradually that we came to see the war in terms of personal, deeply emotional terms.

From time to time Nefyn men and boys left the Merchant for the Royal Navy and sported their smart uniforms whilst home on leave. Some, like my future uncle Ellis Hugh Williams, did a stretch in mine-sweepers and later in Q-boats. Others were drafted into the army. My uncle Idris, who like so many others lied about his age and volunteered at the age of 17, spent only a few weeks in a transit camp before being sent to France to serve on the Somme as a medical orderly and stretcher-bearer. One memorable figure in khaki was Ellis Hugh's brother, David Williams. A tall, strapping young man, he joined the cavalry, carried a leather stick and wore spurs, which meant that he not only looked magnificent but also clinked sweetly as he walked. I cannot recall his face, but I remember his legs very clearly, as I saw them far oftener than the rest of him. This was because Robert 'Dolwen' and I were usually playing marbles when he happened to strut by, and, as soon as we heard the tinkling of spurs and the thudding of heels, we would turn our heads far enough to catch a glimpse of shiny black boots with silver clamps on their heels, topped by a pair of puttied pillars on the move. Marbles seem to figure prominently in my recollections of these days, for Robert and I were having another game at the foot of the old Midland Bank steps (long since demolished) when he paused halfway through a shot, looked up, and told me with a hint of awe in his voice that Evan 'Tŷ Canol' had been drowned. Evan was an A.B. on *HMS Hampshire* which sank with heavy loss of life whilst carrying Lord Kitchener to Russia in an effort to prop up the Tsarist war machine. Kitchener too was dead, but that seemed relatively unimportant at the time.

Young though we were, we were not wholly unacquainted with death in its harsher forms. My first brush with personal tragedy came on a morning shortly before the war when we heard that Mr William Mona Hughes, 'Town Hall', had been killed in the Gwylwyr under sudden fall of rock. It was as though a cloud had fallen upon the village, and everyone spoke in whispers. But, as the grisly war wound on, such individual tragedies began to occur with sickening regularity and at times with frightening speed. Two examples stand out most bleakly in my mind. The wife of Captain Griffith 'Bodwyn' watched him sail from one of the Bristol Channel ports and then caught a train for Pwllheli. Waiting for her when she arrived in 'Bodwyn' was a telegram from the owners with the news that her husband's ship had gone down with all hands . . . One day Father took us, with Captain Griffith 'Llysarborth' and his two small boys (Richard and William John), to a circus in 'Cae John Bull', where the whole party, prompted mainly by Captain Griffith, enjoyed a hilarious afternoon. A few days later he left home to join his ship *S.S. Semantha* in Garston, to take on a cargo of munitions for the troops in the Middle East. The next news that we received of him was that the *Semantha* had been torpedoed without warning north of Alexandria, with a loss of 32 lives (including the Master) . . . As a family we felt those two losses more keenly than most, since they involved two of my father's closest friends, but there were many others to remind even the youngest and most resilient of us that we were caught up in something more than a romantic interlude.

Now and again a flash of better news would help to lighten the gloom. Among those whom we had especial cause to remember, Captain Owen 'Bay View', who lived two doors away from us, was decorated for playing a successful game of hide and seek with a U-boat; and Captain Williams 'Min-y-môr ('Uncle John drws nesa', who was married to Father's sister Jane Mary) was praised in despatches because, after his three-masted barque *Conway Castle* had been sunk in the Pacific on the 27th February 1915, some 560 miles S.W. of Valparaiso, by the German cruiser *Dresden*, he gave the Admiralty such precise information about the raider's whereabouts that Royal Navy units were able to locate, hunt, and destroy her.

We also had some light-hearted moments. We were not a militant community, and the nearest approach to an outburst of sabre-rattling in my experience occurred at a meeting held in the School one Saturday afternoon. A talk on the value of Thrift by Mr Tom Jones 'Hafan' (Manager of the Midland Bank) was followed by a music recital arranged by Mr Harry Owen 'Erw Goch', a marine engineer who was home on leave from the China Seas and had brought along his gramophone, together with a wide selection of appropriate records. The most popular item that day was a patriotic ditty which went with a swing and culminated in the unforgettable chorus:

> 'From the north and the south and the east and the west
> We're going to kill the Kaiser Bill before we take a rest.
> We're going to do our very very very very best
> From the north, south, east, and west.'

Each time that the chorus came round, Harry Owen scanned us with eagle eyes, and, when he raised his hand imperiously, we responded with gusto.

For obvious reasons, sailing ships were pathetically vulnerable to attack. Most U-boat commanders considered them such easy prey that they disdained the use of torpedoes as an un-necessary expense. Instead, they preferred to surface and then to sink the ship either by detonating bombs placed aboard or by gunfire directed below the water-line.

By a mixture of good luck and good management, Father's ship the *Belford* survived the early part of the War without a scratch, and by the summer of 1916 she was loading barley for home in San Francisco, where Father spent much time with relatives and friends. Several snapshots (including one taken in the grounds of Stanford

University) show him with members of the Roberts family – Taid's sister, her husband, and their son. Two other families named Phillips and Hughes (daughters and sons-in-law of the Robertses) appear in picnic groups in the Golden Gate Park and in pictures taken aboard ship. In those snapshots, Father and his apprentices seem relaxed and even cheerful, with nothing to suggest that they faced a nightmare voyage down the West Coast, round the Horn, and up into Atlantic waters – a period of about 3 months during which they would be a sitting target for any hostile marauder lucky enough to catch them in its sights.

There had been a period early in the war when some German commanders tended to adopt an old-fashioned, chivalrous attitude towards their victims. When the *Penrhyn Castle* was stopped by the *Dresden* – a prelude, as a rule, to certain death – she was spared and allowed to set a course for home when the German commander found that her Master, Captain T.J. Evans of Criccieth, had his wife and child on board. Such examples of clemency were by no means uncommon. But by 1917 the long-drawn-out fighting had caused feelings on both sides to harden, and the latest breed of U-boat hunters preferred to wage what came to be known as 'unrestricted warfare'. 'Atrocities' became the order of the day, and even Hospital Ships were not immune, as the *Dover Castle* found to her cost on the 26th May when, 50 miles North from Bona, she was torpedoed without warning and went down with a loss of 5 lives. Some months later the *Llandovery Castle* suffered a similar fate, west of Fastnet, and a total of 146 were either killed or drowned. Some idea of the scale of U-boat attacks in 1917 may be gathered from the fact that in one month, at the climax of the War, 169 merchant vessels (representing a tonnage of well over half a million) were sunk, and 1,125 lives were lost.

What the Americans thought of the *Belford*'s chances is made clear enough in a news item which was sent from San Francisco to the newspaper *The Welsh American*, formerly *The Druid*, of Pittsburgh, Pennsylvania. It starts:

> 'When the good Welsh ship *Belford*, commanded by the genial Captain William Davies of Nevin, North Wales, sailed from this port on August 23, it was feared that she would not be able to reach her destination.'

How right they were! By early February 1917 she had arrived 100 miles west of Fastnet (Latitude 50.34 North, Longitude 12.16 West) when she was stopped by a U-boat. The German commander ordered the crew to take their boats, and peremptorily refused to allow them to salvage any of their belongings. The only article which Father managed to rescue was his telescope.

It did not take long to dispose of the *Belford*, and, although Father never cared to dwell upon the episode, he admitted that seeing her go down slowly, bow first, and with her poop high in the air, was one of the saddest moments of his life.

When they had taken to the boats, the German commander insisted upon towing them inshore. Father questioned his motives but was in no position to refuse. The boats were therefore roped together and tied to the U-boat. The carpenter sat in the bow of the leading boat, with instructions to use his axe at the first sign of danger. After working up a good speed the U-boat suddenly dived, with the clear intention of dragging the boats down with it, but the ropes parted and the axe was not needed.

Having spent over 48 hours adrift in dirty weather, they were picked up by the destroyer *HMS Myosotis* and landed in Bantry Bay. Then on to Dublin and Holyhead, where

Father enjoyed his cousins' hospitality before coming home. The commander of the *Myosotis* had given him two ribbons to be worn by my brother and myself on our sailors' hats, and we took great pride in them, as they were, for a change, the real thing.

The company's letter reporting the loss of the *Belford* is dated the 3rd February 1917 and reads: 'Pleased to state that all the crew were saved... It has been decided not to replace the ship but to wind up the company... In the event of winding up, we hope that each £50 Share Capital invested will realise about £300.'

When Father arrived by train at Pwllheli, we took the parrot along for company, and, much to the amusement of the other bus passengers, my brother insisted on relieving the tedium of the journey from Nefyn by bawling 'Hen hogia'n dwad adra heno' to the tune of 'See the Conquering Hero comes'.

Father's arrival was both a delight and a shock, for the first thing that struck us was that he had lost the moustache which had until then seemed an integral part of him. He must have seen the surprise on our faces, for he took immediate pains to explain that the U-boat commander had released him only on condition that he shaved off his moustache for the duration of the war. In fact, he remained clean-shaven for the rest of his life. We accepted his story without question and resigned ourselves to the new look as a small price to pay for having him safely home once again.

One change when Father was at home was that life became more varied and eventful. Many a morning, at some unearthly hour, he would call me out of bed to go sailing with him and his friends; more people than usual called at the house; friends and acquaintances of all kinds came to supper. There were also sing-songs which started early in the evening and continued for hours. On such occasions we were packed off to bed with strict orders to lie low, but the excitement of wondering what was going on made sleep unwelcome, and we tried our best to recognise the voice of each visitor as he or she arrived. Prominent among the singers was Evan Jones 'Old Post', whose bell-like tenor voice was easily distinguishable once the festivities were under way, and who will always be associated in my mind with such popular stand-by's as 'The Holy City', 'The Lost Chord', 'Myfanwy', or 'A Life on the Ocean Wave'. As the concert wound on, we would slowly venture out of bed and kneel furtively against the landing-rail in the hope of salvaging something from the buzz of conversation, the gusts of laughter, and the gentle tinkling of tea-cups which emanated from below during the intervals, but it was never very long before sleep took over and drove us back between the sheets.

Apart from one or two visits to Liverpool, presumably in search of another ship, Father remained at home for the next few months while the war dragged its slow length along. For some reason or other, we accompanied him on one of those visits and caught glimpses of both the seamy and the glittering sides of city life.

One day, while we were playing in a park in Bootle, with Mother reading on a bench nearby, I was approached by an elderly man who had a toddler by the hand and who asked me to keep an eye on the child while he went to buy tobacco. Some time later, when Mother called us to join her, the man had still not returned, so we took the child along and explained what had happened. Mother at once suspected the worst, and turned for help to the only other adult in sight, an exceptionally tall man wearing dark clothes and a broad-brimmed black hat. He quickly sized up the situation, and in no time at all our poor young friend was being carried away under protest in the arms of a burly policeman . . . The tall man, as Mother knew, was the Rev. Peter Williams, otherwise known as Pedr Hir, and author of the well-known hymn:

> 'Bydd canu yn y nefoedd
> Pan ddelo'r saint ynghyd . . . '

According to the 'Bywgraffiadur', he served as Baptist Minister in Bootle for a quarter century, and died there in 1922.

In complete contrast to the seedy life which that sad little episode reflected were the cinemas which we saw in the heart of Liverpool. Those lush palaces, with their whispering violins, potted palms, vast stairways and soft, deep carpets, were like glimpses of El Dorado to boys brought up on the bleakness of the Madryn Hall and who regarded the Town Hall in Pwllheli as the last word in sophisticated refinement. When we returned home to Nefyn after such revelations, we ceased to be sailors for a while and became cowboys, using the beach as a Western prairie, chasing each other up and down the cliff face, shooting it out with imaginery Winchesters or '45s among the rocks of Creigiau Mawr, or cantering away on some errand of mercy along tracks drawn by pram-wheels in the sand.

That trip to Liverpool was the only journey of any length which we made during the war. Otherwise, on the rare occasions when we left home, it was to call on friends in such places as Llithfaen, Trefor, or Pwllheli. One of Taid's oldest friends in Llithfaen was Aidan Davies. Not only were they both quarrymen; together they had played a leading part in building the first Congregational chapel in Llithfaen, where previous meetings had been held in barns and private houses. The Aidan Davies whom I came to know was like a benevolent bear, with a massive, powerful frame, and a gentle, selfless disposition. At one period he made a point of leaving home each morning about half an hour earlier than necessary so that he could devote that time to erecting a stone barrier for the benefit of travellers who might be caught in rough weather on the mountain side and who would be glad of some shelter, however primitive. The work took several months to complete . . . He also taught himself First Aid so that he could help injured men in the quarry, and often spent so much time attending to the needs of others that he had hardly any money to take home on the fortnightly pay-day. Llithfaen was such a closely-knit community that his friends would never have willingly allowed him or his family to suffer, but some suffering was inevitable, and I remember being taken to Llithfaen to a 'Cyfarfod Ysgol' one brilliant Whit Sunday, calling at the Aidan Davies home, and seeing a young boy scarcely older than myself, whose face was almost as white as the cloth on the table by his side. A few weeks later he died of T.B. According to the headstone on his grave, the year was 1917.

For us, the end of the War came quietly, and was preceded by the inevitable spate of rumours. One day the postman walked into Canton House to announce categorically that a German submarine had run aground somewhere on the Isle of Man and that the entire crew had surrendered because they were 'sicken tired of the War' – or so it sounded to me. Then came a Sunday afternoon when Captain Jones 'Cemlyn' dropped in with the news that the fighting was at long last over. There was no hint of jubilation, only a deep sense of relief, persistent niggling doubts, and an undramatic acceptance of whatever the future might hold.

Some months later, on one of my regular trips to the Bakery at Alun House, Mr Thomas Williams showed himself to be a shopkeeper with a sense of history by drawing my attention to a poster, hanging inside the door, which showed pictures of two aviators, named Alcock and Brown, together with the plane in which they had just flown the Atlantic from West to East. Mr Williams considered this to be the finest feat of endurance since Captain Webb's exploit in swimming the Channel, and he hinted that they might even follow the good Captain's example by having their names and pictures immortalised on a match-box. I am not aware that his prophecy was ever fulfilled.

10

Aftermath of War

Not all the tragic events which punctuated the period 1914-1918 were due to the war. One of our near neighbours, young J . . . , suffered tribulations which had nothing to do directly with the Kaiser or with anyone else outside his own family.

When his mother died suddenly whilst his father (a native of Eifionydd) was away at sea, the latter's two sisters came to Nefyn to fill the vacuum and to keep the house ticking over. They were not an attractive pair. One was short and bent, the other tall and rigid, but they were both equally aloof, unsmiling, and (to a child) indefinably sinister as they swept and flitted silently about the place in their long black clothes, looking for all the world like two birds of ill omen or like two fugitives from the darker pages of the Grimm brothers' Fairy Tales.

From the first they made it clear that they wished to have no truck with the natives, and even erected a high wooden fence between themselves and the house next door. I found it a disturbing experience to have two such chilly characters so close at hand. Not for many years did I discover that their appearance was not the worst thing about them.

For some reason which no one outside their own circle has ever been able to fathom, they decided that young J was a ne'er-do-well who deserved no better treatment from his father than to be cut off with the proverbial shilling. Their powers of persuasion must have been strong, for it took them only a few months of steady letter-writing to achieve their mission.

In the meantime J . . . reached military age. He was duly drafted into the army, and, after the Armistice of November 1918, joined the occupation forces in Cologne. When he first came home on leave, he knew nothing of his aunts' activities, and was therefore totally unprepared for the welcome which awaited him. Travelling from London on the overnight Mail train he arrived in Nefyn in the early morning. When he reached the house, it was locked and empty, but in the lavatory at the back he found an old pillow-case in which were a crumpled suit of clothes and an envelope containing a ten-shilling note. His neighbours had to tell him that the house had been sold and all its contents auctioned, that his two aunts had returned to Eifionydd, and that there was no news of his father. In fact, he and his father did not meet again until the early 1930s. It would be interesting to know what they talked about.

* * *

It must have been about the same time that Father took me with him to the Madryn Hall to hear Lloyd George. To the boys of my generation L.G. was a familiar but remote figure, the stuff of which legends are made. We knew that he was Prime Minister in the same way as we knew that Jack Dempsey was heavyweight champion of the world, and we took it for granted that both of them, the Welsh Wizard and the Manassa Mauler, were simply and incontrovertibly the best of their kind. On special occasions, when we gave the matter any thought, we were also proud of the fact that L.G. was our M.P. (whatever that meant), and during one election campaign I remember prancing around the school yard with a number of other boys, chanting:

'Lloyd George ar ben y pôl,
Lloyd George ar ben y pôl,
Ac Austin yn y gwaelod
Yn byta licismôl'.

Those rousing words were sung to variations on the last few bars of 'Mae gen i ddafad gorniog'. The Austin in question was presumably either Austin Harrison or Austin Jones, both of whom opposed L.G. in post-war elections – needless to say, without success. The newspapers of course always carried photographs of our hero, but before that historic visit to the Madryn Hall I had never seen him in the flesh.

The place was full to over-flowing; people crowded in the doorways and even stood precariously on the window-ledges. As we waited for his arrival, we were entertained by two amusing speakers from Holyhead – R. J. Thomas the sitting member for the island, and a doctor who made jokes about 'panel patients', an expression which went right over my head but for some reason brought roars of approval from the audience. Then he arrived, and, after the hubbub which greeted his arrival had subsided, he began to speak. Even as a young boy, I immediately felt the ebullience, the sense of fun, and the charm that radiated from him. Above all, I remember what I can only describe as a superb display of creative oratory, the like of which I had never seen before. 'Seen' is the word, for the effect upon me was visual in the sense that he compelled me to see what he was doing. What he did in fact was to build a bridge, the bridge of Freedom, and he built it arch by arch – freedom of conscience, freedom of assembly, freedom of speech, freedom of the press, and so on down the ages until it stood almost complete. Almost but not quite. One more arch was needed to complete it so that we could cross it in our search for a better life – the arch of Free Trade. I do not recall a single phrase that he used, but that afternoon, in a drab and stuffy little hall, he achieved the miracle of making that bridge materialise almost literally before my eyes – an exhilarating, breath-taking experience.

A less conventional impression was made upon us by a young man who flashed into prominence after the War and became, for a time at least, a topic of conversation in every house in the area. This was Tomi 'Bodeilias', whose home was a smallholding on the seaward slope of the Gwylwyr, with a grandstand view of Caernarfon Bay and beyond. His brothers, Hughes and John, answered the call of the sea and became Master Mariners, but Tomi heard other voices. His father, John Williams, was an old friend of my grandfather, John Owen; he was also, nominally, a farmer cum carpenter, but in practice he spent most of his time either writing verse or playing the violin, and, on Sundays, serving as lay preacher to the various denominations which needed his services. Tomi soon showed that he had inherited some of his father's gifts in a highly concentrated form. After serving in the Army on the Somme and in Gallipoli, and suffering heavy internal wounds from which he never fully recovered, he returned home to Bodeilias determined to preach the gospel of peace and good will to all men. For such a task he was well equipped, with a compelling voice and personality, an intense manner, and a natural eloquence which never degenerated into hollow rhetoric. Not content with working within the formal limits of Chapel and Sunday, he became also an itinerant preacher, setting up his pulpit on week-day evenings in such unlikely places as Y Groes, near the front door of the Sportsman Hotel, on the cliffs overlooking Lôn Gam, or among the gravestones in the 'new cemetery'. There we would sometimes join the crowd which listened intently to him as he read portions of the Bible, led the hymn-singing in his rich bass voice, then prayed and preached in tones which could be heard ringing a long way off. Even now, over 60 years later, I can still hear him declaiming in a voice which both appealed and threatened: 'Nid meudwy mo Iesu Grist. Gwir y carai'r encilion . . . ' and so on. Some of the boys were convinced that he must be a true prophet in the Biblical sense, for their parents had heard him correctly predict the dire fate which awaited, and which soon afterwards befell, certain individuals who had most blatantly defied the laws of God . . . Some of us found him useful as a pretext for staying out late. More than once we followed him to such remote outposts as Capel y Mynydd, where the congregation had overflowed to such an extent that we could not even reach the door. But, although he amazed and intrigued us, we cannot pretend that he made any lasting impression upon our young minds. He was, quite simply, a phenomenon which we instantly recognised as extraordinary but were wholly incapable of understanding. In time, he went away and temporarily vanished from our lives, and some years were to elapse before we discovered that he had become known throughout Wales as 'Tom Nefyn'.

11

The Monkbarns

With the coming of peace in 1918, life gradually became far less constrained, as though steel gates which had hemmed us in for four years were at long last flung wide open. The relief which we felt may not have been dramatic, but it was none the less real, and it was wonderful to reflect that, when Father resumed his life at sea, we no longer had to think of his movements in terms of U-boats and other hostile craft.

One post-war development of direct consequence to us was that the Robert Thomas company decided to wind up its affairs. Robert Thomas himself had died before the War, and it might well be that, without his controlling hand, the company would sooner rather than later have died a natural death. The War accelerated the process by causing grave losses to the Thomas fleet. Whereas in the first decade of the century it consisted of some 15 vessels – ranging in size from the *Gwrtheyrn Castle* (778/803 tons) to the *Rhuddlan Castle* (1993/2093 tons) – by 1918 natural wastage had combined with German ruthlessness to reduce that number to six. Not surprisingly, therefore, Robert Thomas' son, Robert Rees Thomas, and his fellow directors decided that they had had enough, and all their ships which had survived the War were sold. This development left Father with no option but to join some other company, and, since he was determined to remain in sail, his choice was of necessity limited.

He had the following reference to help him:

> 34, State Insurance Buildings
> 14 Dale Street
> Liverpool
> 30th February 1919.

TO WHOM IT MAY CONCERN:

'This is to certify that the bearer, Captain William Davies, has served continuously in our employ for twenty-three (23) years from January 1884 to February 1917 as Master of our Barques *'Eivion'*, *'Gwrtheyrn Castle'*, *'Gwydyr Castle'*, and sailing ship *'Belford'*. We have disposed of all our ships and are therefore unable to offer him further employment. He is absolutely reliable and sober, and we do not know of a more capable shipmaster. He always made good passages and incurred very little damage; expedited the work of the ships in port and was very economical in disbursements. We strongly recommend Captain Davies to anyone requiring his services, and shipping property entrusted to his experienced hands means a minimum of anxiety to his employer.

(SD) R. Thomas & Co.'

Fortunately he did not have long to wait, for in June 1919 he was summoned to Cork to take command of the *Monkbarns*, a steel full-rigger of 1,771 registered tons, belonging to John Stewart of London. John Stewart's main office was at Nos. 26-28 Billiter Street, described by A. J. Villiers as 'the last of the English square-riggers' headquarters'.[11]

The *Monkbarns* was two years younger than the *Gwydyr Castle*, having been built in 1895 by MacMillans of Dumbarton. A few years ago Captain Bruce Glasier, who had good reason to know her, commissioned a painting of her by the artist Mark Richard Myers, and until quite recently this picture figured in the Cape Horn Gallery of the National Maritime Museum at Greenwich. Its temporary disappearance from view is due to the fact that the old Cape Horn Gallery no longer exists in its original form, but there are indications that the Myers painting of the old ship may soon re-appear in some fresh setting.

(This picture may now be viewed at: https://collections.rmg.co.uk/collections/objects/14971.html).

Her over-all record, embracing more than thirty years, contained the familiar mixture of good fortune and near-disaster. Off Cape Horn in 1909 she was trapped in an ice field for 63 days, and, although she eventually sailed clear when the weather warmed, the experience cost the life of the master, and many of her crew only narrowly escaped being frozen to death.

By contrast, during the 1914-1918 War she led a charmed life, often escaping imminent catastrophe in a way which temporarily gained her the title of 'the lucky *Monkbarns*'. Once, she spotted the enemy cruisers *Scharnhorst, Gneisenau, Leipzig,* and *Dresden,* but they ignored her because they had more important matters on their mind, since they were on their way towards the Falkland Islands to fight British units in an engagement which was to become known as the Battle of Coronel. Some months later, she was only five miles away from the *Lusitania* when the ill-fated Cunarder was torpedoed by a U-boat and sank with the loss of 1,500 lives.

By June 1919 she had just completed a series of voyages which began in February 1917 and which kept her away from the United Kingdom for two years and four months. Although the final stages of this long odyssey were completed in peace-time, they were by no means uneventful, for, while she was on the 16,000-mile run from

Melbourne to New York with a cargo of flour, some members of her crew fell foul of their officers and mutinied. For 3 long months her 76-year-old master, Captain Donaldson, and the loyal members of her crew held out against a fractious group who seized every opportunity to foment trouble by exploiting the slightest grievance. They began by complaining that the food was inedible, as the potatoes were black and the peas as hard as marbles. Since all ships were having to survive as best they could on wartime rations, there was some ground for their complaint; but it soon became evident that they were not simply concerned with righting wrongs and that a full-scale mutiny was coming to the boil. One day 6 seamen stormed the poop, cornered Captain Donaldson in the chart-room, pinned him against the table and threatened him with their knives. The officers arrived in time to prevent any bloodshed, but the captain decided to take no further chances, and, when they came within range of Rio de Janeiro, he flew a distress signal and made for port, where the mutineers were court-martialled and sentenced. There too the ship disposed of the cargo ear-marked for New York before sailing to Cape Town to pick up a load of grain for Ireland . . . It was at the end of this stirring voyage that Captain Donaldson retired and that Father took his place.

The official historian of the John Stewart Line, Captain A. G. Course, sums up the story of her life in these words: 'The *Monkbarns* was one of the most famous vessels of the John Stewart fleet. She was a lovely ship but had more than her share of bad weather and bad luck'[12] . . . Judged by the standards of the *Gwydyr*, she may have been no oil-painting, for, while the former belonged to the age of the semi-clippers, the *Monkbarns* was built primarily, if not exclusively, as a carrier; and some ancient mariners, in their prouder moments, were inclined to refer to such ships as 'boxes'. Even so, she was not only 'a lovely ship' but also a handy one, for she had many labour-saving devices for working the sails and the cargo. Moreover, her living quarters were spacious, attractive, and comparatively luxurious. As Frank C. Bowen puts it in his *Ships of London River*, 'she had comfortable quarters both forward and aft, and her owners had spared no expense in decorating her with really fine teak on deck and below'[13] . . . Her figure-head, a white flying-horse, gave her powerful bows a touch of distinction, and, although she never pretended to be a flyer herself, she had the reputation of being a tough, solid performer who could be relied upon not to waste time.

This was in sharp contrast to her sister ship the *William Mitchell*, which, despite the fact that she was built to the same specifications, made a habit of being overdue, and more than once was given up for lost. It so happens that the Mate of the *Monkbarns*, Captain Stewart Wilkie, left early in 1920 to take command of the *William Mitchell*, and he had no better luck than his predecessors. On 6th October of that year she left Gulfport for Buenos Aires where she was expected to arrive by Christmas. Instead, she crossed the Equator 13 times in her efforts to get there, and temporarily disappeared from sight, re-appearing on the 2nd March 1921 when she put into Barbados, 147 days out. Having replenished her stores, she moved on 4 days later, but did not reach Buenos Aires until the 29th June, the voyage having taken no less than 266 days. This achievement stands as the British all-time record for that particular run.

The new-found freedom which we enjoyed after the Armistice became apparent when my mother, sister, and brother went over to Cork to join Father. I was also invited, but had reached the stage where I preferred to stay at home with one of my aunts so that I could go on playing with my friends, for I failed to see how any other place could possibly offer such amenities as those which lay on my own doorstep. More particularly, I was eager to indulge a taste for sailing and fishing which Father had kindled during his recent months at home. The result was that, while the other members of the family cavorted along Irish lanes in jaunting-cars or made pilgrimages to such traditional shrines as Tipperary and Killarney, it was in a more familiar setting that I celebrated the first full summer of peace and found myself so fully occupied that I had no time to miss them.

One rich bonus which unexpectedly came my way was the arrival on the scene of a future uncle, Captain Owen Robyns Owen of Llanbedrog, who spent most of his time on the China station. He was shortly to marry my aunt Myfanwy, and I was already aware of his existence, for whenever she was around, the talk was liberally peppered with such names as Shanghai, Hong Kong, Singapore, and Penang, which at least made a change from the West Coast.

When he arrived home on leave, he used to travel to Nefyn almost every day to take his future wife for a spin on his motorbike – an enormous maroon-coloured Indian, complete with open side-car in which my aunt sat with a voluminous veil about her head, looking for all the world as though she had just emerged from a bee-hive. Much to my joy and amazement, they often invited me to accompany them as an extra passenger, on the pillion, no doubt casting me in the role of unobtrusive chaperone. Among the pleasures which we enjoyed in this style were sports meetings at Pwllheli, Sarn, and Efailnewydd. For me, such visits represented riches far beyond the dreams of avarice, for one of our special delights after the war was to watch the running of William John Williams of Efailnewydd, a recent member of the RFC/RAF and a close friend of our uncle Idris.

In face and build, Wil John was a miniature Georges Carpentier. A natural athlete, he moved like a greyhound both in the sprints and over the middle distances, and, whenever he ran, he won with such ease and regularity that his opponents always insisted upon a handicap, which he readily conceded but which never made the slightest difference to the outcome. He appeared to toy with the opposition, lurking in the rear of the field and nonchalantly biding his time until they approached the final bend, then accelerating like a rocket and leaving his rivals for dead. With his 'effortless superiority' he might have come straight out of the pages of Boys' Own . . . Only once did I see him lose a race, and that was in his home village of Efailnewydd, where he entered the Mile and trotted around for a few laps, ostensibly following his usual tactic of watching the enemy from behind. Then, to my horror, he stopped and calmly walked off the track, leaving the race to be won by a dark curly-haired young Aberystwyth student from Llanaelhaearn. At the time I felt not only disappointed but betrayed, as Wil John had led us to believe in his invincibility as an article of faith, and it was scant comfort to be told by him afterwards that he had had more than his share of success and that it was high time for the younger athletes to start winning a few races. The name of the winner on that particular day was Lambert Gapper.

Not all my memories of that first post-war summer are happy ones. Local habits die hard, and the old custom which had compelled my uncle Idris to fight every boy of his age still operated in my time. I have good cause to remember one new boy called David Roberts, who came to be known as Dai *Sportsman*. One fine evening a group of us watched the Roberts family and their belongings arrive at the *Sportsman Hotel* on a large lorry which was drawn by a pair of majestic horses, gleaming with brass and good health, and each carrying between his ears a tiny bell which tinkled melodiously as he dipped or reared his head. In the family were three boys, two of approximately our age, and we wondered what they were like. We soon found out, for a couple of days later it fell to my lot to fight Dai outside the *Glynllifon* warehouse in *Cae Rhyg*. 'Fight' is hardly the word, as Dai proved himself to be a lethal blend of wildcat and tornado, ruthlessly proceeded to pound every part of my body which he could reach, and within minutes had reduced me to the level of a zombie. By the time the 'fight' was stopped, I was filthy with dust, one eye was firmly closed, my whole body ached, and my head buzzed like a dynamo. On the way home I tottered into Brynhyfryd to repair some of the damage, and Nain, after taking one look at me, made sympathetic noises and was close to tears as she placed a bowl on the table and took the kettle off the hob. Taid lowered his copy of the *Daily News* and removed his pipe before peering at my face, but his only reaction was a brief snort and the comment: 'He'll be lucky if that's the worst that ever happens to him' – a remark which struck me at the time as both irrelevant and callous.

Dai and I were to become quite friendly, although he remained far too unpredictable for comfort. Playing with him was like having a tiger as a pet, and once at least he tried his best to persuade me to run away with him, although he had no idea where he wanted to go. A long afternoon spent in vain attempts to catch pigeons in the huge barns of Portinllaen Farm served to put an effective damper on his wanderlust, and he reluctantly agreed to come home for the night. It must be admitted that life became less trying when soon afterwards the Roberts family moved elsewhere to live.

---

[11] A. J. Villiers, *Sea Dogs of Today* (1932), p. 66.

[12] Capt. A. G. Course, *The Wheel's Kick and the Wind's Song* (3rd ed. 1968), facing p. 147.

[13] Frank C. Bowen, *Sailing Ships of the London River* (n.d.) p. 205.

Hugh Davies the Nailer, who taught more than one generation of Nefyn boys the elements of Navigation.

Part of the crowd which attended the funeral of the men lost on the North Anglia.

(above and opposite) Ship Monkbarns *becalmed.*

January 1920. Monkbarns being towed up the Avon, with the Clifton suspension bridge in the background.

Crew of the Monkbarns on the eve of leaving Birkenhead for Sydney, N.S.W., March 1923. Among the group standing on the deck are: On the extreme left of the viewer, Capt. Richard Davies (then Mate), on the extreme right Capt. M.B. Glasier (then Third Mate), and waving a trilby hat, Capt. W.H. Hughes (then Able Seaman). At the back with my father is a R.N. Commander, who was making the trip for the good of his health.

above: After the hurricane, when the weather had moderated and the sea was relatively calm. Picture taken from the fore part of the poop lee-side. The line of the horizon gives some idea of the extent to which the ship had listed.

right: Picture taken from the lee fore yard-arm.

Taken from the brink of the poop, weather side. Here again the horizon shows the angle of tilt.

A week after being struck by a hurricane, the Monkbarns *limps into Cape Town for repairs. Picture taken by the 'Cape Argus'.*

Author's Note:
It was Captain Glasier who generously placed at my disposal his wonderful collection of pictures of the Monkbarns.

12

Discovering Nefyn

It was during those early post-war years that I became increasingly aware of my surroundings and began to appreciate how lucky I was to be brought up in such an idyllic spot. Quite apart from the natural beauty of the place, there was also a strong sense of belonging to a closely-knit community with a long and vigorous past.

It came as a surprise to me in later years to discover that Pwllheli people regarded us as 'clannish', for I saw no trace of the exclusiveness which must characterise any clan system. On the contrary, our particular 'clan' included a generous share of 'importations', a name commonly given to men who had come in from the outside because they were attracted by the prospect of using Nefyn as a base either for going to sea or for working in the local quarry. Once those 'importations' had been absorbed, they became an integral part of the population, and inter-marriages accelerated the process. Only their names remained as a faded token of the original differences. In my young days, such names as Dobson, Cooke, Wilson, and Nicholson had been part of the scene for generations, and the more exotic Baum, Olsen, and Swingler came as trippingly off the tongue as Jones, Williams, or Davies.

Tangible evidence of the vigorous past was still there for all to see. Over in Portinllaen, the jetty and storehouses where David Richard used to call with his pony and trap were monuments to the activity and determination of the last century. So were the ribs of some abandoned hulks slowly disintegrating near Creigiau Bach . . . Places like 'Tŷ

Coch' and 'Whitehall' hinted excitingly at the good old days when the area was a happy hunting ground for smugglers, and private houses with names like 'The Bull', 'Newborough', and 'White Horse' recalled a period when Nefyn had many more pubs than chapels . . . We could actually talk to people whose parents remembered that dreadful day in 1859 when the small schooner *Revival*, then under construction at Portinllaen, was battered and blown off the stocks by the same storm as destroyed the *Royal Charter*: many more could tell us that they had been present on the beach when the schooner *Venus*, the last ship to be built at Nefyn, had been launched to the accompaniment of loud cheers way back in 1880. The same people also recalled the days when herring catches in the bay were so heavy that enormous stacks of unwanted fish piled up in Cae Rhyg, to be finally disposed of as manure. The more pious amongst us even hinted that the subsequent shortage of herring must be a punishment meted out to us as a community for our previous greed and prodigality.

But, as parents and teachers were quick to point out, our links with the past went back much further than that. Whenever we returned from a fishing trip and dropped anchor in the bay, we were only doing what Welsh princes like Gruffydd ap Cynan had done many times on their return voyages from Dublin, when contrary winds prevented them from making Abermenai . . . When we walked along Stryd Plas, we stepped on ground once occupied by the principal royal seat in Lleyn . . . When we caught tadpoles and tiddlers in the stream at Bryn-mynach, we were close to the site where, eight centuries earlier, Gerald the Welshman rested on his way to Bardsey, spending the night at the Priory as a guest of the monks . . . When we trudged beyond Fron Fawr towards the Garn and looked down upon a field shaped remarkably like a herring, with a small clump of trees to mark the eye, we saw the meadow where in 1283 Edward Ist held a famous tournament modelled on the Round Table; and on the Garn itself we played among a number of circular grass-covered remains, which had been there since the dawn of history and were known as *Cytiau Gwyddelod*. All these relics and folk-memories and myths formed part of the background against which we grew up.

As growing boys, however, we had no time to reflect on such matters, for we were far more interested in the present than the past, and the present had much to commend it. It was naturally on the beach or in the bay that we preferred to spend our time, but in other places too there was plenty to stir our interest, and no account of our salad days would be complete without some reference to them.

To say that the more formal games which we played included both soccer and cricket would be misleading. For us, soccer usually meant kicking a small rubber ball on the school yard or on any other open space which happened to be available; and cricket meant wielding a small plank or a thick stick to protect a large tin can which was placed in the middle of the road and which had to be moved to make room for passing carts or cows. On the rare days when we plucked up enough courage to play in a field, we always took the precaution of posting a look-out on top of the hedge so that we could be warned of approaching danger. For both games, we made up the rules as we went along. There were among us one or two pedants whose parents provided them with expensive Annuals and who therefore referred in learned terms to the FA and the MCC, but their views, although interesting, were dismissed as irrelevant. Ignorance is a great leveller.

An authentic football was an almost priceless rarity in those days, for few of us could afford to pay the necessary price, and we often relied for help in this direction on young sailors who came home on leave and found that they had a few shillings to invest. Failing such sponsors, we tried to make-do with such substitutes as bladders from the carcasses of dead animals. These we obtained by offering our services to Fred, the butcher who worked in the slaughterhouse at the back of the premises known as 'Siop Cig Rhad', so called because it was the first shop in Nefyn to sell imported lamb. During working hours, when Fred was not in the slaughterhouse, he was likely to be found travelling bare-back on a grey pony, with a large basket on his left arm, carrying deliveries to out-lying customers. The rest of his time he spent in one of the local pubs.

This was a pity, for drink had proved to be the undoing of Fred's father. On his way home from a carousal in Pwllheli, his horse had thrown him as he approached Boduan Hill, and, with his foot trapped in the stirrup, he had been dragged to his death.

When Fred was under the influence, he could be both surly and unpredictable, and there was a legend that, on one wet Saturday night, after a long session at the bar, he had ridden his pony through the front door of 'Siop Cig Rhad' and tried to steer it upstairs. When he was sober, he could be amiable enough, in a subdued way, and as a rule he welcomed our offers to help him with his work. Such help consisted of going to one corner of the slaughterhouse and hanging like grim death to one end of a long rope which passed through a block in the high ceiling, while, somewhere out of sight, Fred went about his deadly work. In practice, our role in this grisly operation was not as callous as it sounds, since we were far too busy to become emotionally involved. Our eyes were glued exclusively on the rope and the block, and no thoughts of ruthless mayhem ever entered our minds.

In return for our collaboration, we could claim the bladder as a reward. Unfortunately for us, most of the bladders in my experience turned out to be a bitter disappointment, by either bursting catastrophically in a matter of minutes or else proving so grotesquely volatile and shapeless that no one could control them.

There were other games, involving the use of spinning tops, hoops, marbles, cigarette cards etc. which all had their separate and distinct seasons. How those seasons came to be defined is a mystery which most of us were never able to fathom, but the fact remains that they followed a consistent pattern, like the coming of primroses or the migration of birds. At about the same time every year, with almost cosmic regularity and with the inevitability of fate, one particular game would suddenly make its appearance, usurp the place of another, flourish for a while, and then as suddenly disappear to make way for its successor. This esoteric calendar had its own conventions, known apparently to a chosen few, which we were all expected to observe, and anyone who was eccentric enough, say, to play marbles during the spinning-top season, or vice versa, was considered very odd indeed. Among the sporting establishment of our day it simply was not done.

One good thing about these activities was that they cost us next to nothing, for we could safely rely on finding such tackle as tops and marbles in our Christmas stockings, and they could be expected to last a long time. Even if a disastrous run of games wiped out one's stock of marbles and taws, it was always possible to borrow a handful from a friend as a first step towards recouping one's losses. All this meant that money, and the habit of spending it, played only a tiny part in our personal calculations. For such special outings as concerts or visits to the 'pictures', we naturally turned for support to our parents or some other patron, but for all other purposes we were expected to survive on the single penny which was formally handed to us on Saturday morning and which was supposed to last one week. As we promptly spent it on a large slab of chocolate or on some garishly coloured liquorice sweets with a name which can have no place in a respectable publication, we spent the remaining six days in a state of blissful penury.

The more mercenary, or the more enterprising, among us had ways of supplementing their basic income. One was to loiter not too far away from the *Post Office* in the hope that there might be a telegram to deliver, more often than not with news of some ship or other. If we were in luck, the plump form of Mr John Ellis Jones the postmaster would sooner or later appear on the doorstep and, with a few shrill blasts on his whistle, incite every small boy within hail to join in a mad race in his direction. The first boy to arrive would be patted on the head, appointed special messenger for the moment, despatched on his errand with the telegram discreetly tucked inside a small black leather case which he could strap on his wrist, and on his return receive the recognised rate for the job. This could be as low as one ha'penny; even for a long uphill trek to Pistyll or Mynydd Nefyn it was never more than tuppence; but for us such sums meant wealth. We were further sustained in our efforts by the prospect of breaking the record for the course.

Our finances were likely to improve out of all recognition when friends or relatives came home on leave, for whenever they met us they automatically dipped their hands in their pockets and gave us one or two brown coins or even a sixpenny bit, with sometimes an odd foreign piece thrown in for good measure. This was a practice which Mother deplored, but there was not much that she could do about it. She was equally helpless when Father was at home and tended to ruin her well-meaning attempts to teach us the elements of personal thrift as understood by our Puritan forebears. I can still recapture the feeling of utter disbelief which came over me when he first gave me half a crown, and the look of mingled horror and resignation on Mother's face when he told her what he had done. This was the only issue on which I ever found my parents to be, even remotely, at variance. Otherwise there was complete harmony between them, for, although in physical appearance they made an interesting contrast – Mother being dark-haired and brown-eyed, Father with light hair and blue eyes – in temperament they were surprisingly similar and clearly in total accord as to how their three children should be brought up. Superficially perhaps Mother might sometimes give us the impression of being the stricter and more unbending of the two, but that was mainly because she was permanently with us and therefore carried the heavier share of the responsibility, whereas Father was to some degree a background figure who, when he intermittently burst into our lives for short glorious spells, brought with him a strong whiff of romance, so that in our attitude to him there was always a touch of hero-worship, and in his attitude to us an inevitable tendency to be indulgent. Essentially, however, both parents were alike, in the sense that they combined kindness and an unobtrusive strength of character to a degree which inspired the affection and loyalty of all who knew them and succeeded in creating for their children a home which remained at all times a warm, secure haven against the uncertainties of childhood and adolescence.

When for some reason we found it impossible to kick a ball around, it was not too difficult to discover other ways of filling our time. We only had to wander in the direction of *Cefn Maes* to find the smithy of Ifan Go', who looked like any other mortal on Sundays and holidays when he was all dressed up, but on working days wore a leather apron which transformed him into a sorcerer, capable of turning a straight steel rod into a boy's hoop in the twinkling of an eye – for the sum of one penny. With luck, we might arrive at the smithy in time to see him shoe a pony or a cart-horse, which he did, like everything else, in calm unhurried fashion. When the preliminaries were over and he had pared the patient's hoof with his razor-sharp knife, it was exciting to watch him move across to the large bellows, pump them until the fire had worked itself into a frenzy, twirl the white-hot shoe on to the anvil so that he could tap it into shape, then, after dipping it briskly into a bucket of cold water, deftly place it on the horse's hoof and nail it home, while the place filled with smoke and steam and the smell of burning horn.

On the way from the smithy in *Cefn Maes* to the lower end of the village at Penisardre, we might stop at any one of three workshops to volunteer our help as floor-sweepers, as an excuse for watching a master joiner at work. In *Tanymaes*, cosily tucked in to a rock at the foot of the stone steps which led to *Penygraig*, was the workshop belonging to Mr Thomas Jones, a trim, gentle man who sometimes allowed us to help but rarely encouraged us to talk. He had a son, Thomas John, who was destined to do well at the Universities of Leipzig and Toronto, and to become known throughout Presbyterian Wales as Dr T. J. Jones, a Minister and a Hebrew scholar of distinction. His last pastorate was in Crwys Road, Cardiff.

Halfway down Well Street was another roomy shed belonging to Mr David Hughes, a burly man whose chief claim to renown in our eyes was the fact that, as a soccer player of outstanding local repute, he had been given a trial by Aston Villa in the palmy days of Sam Hardy, Billy Walker, and Andy Ducat. Unfortunately, he was no more talkative than Mr Jones. This was a pity, for there were many questions which we should have liked to ask him, not only about himself but also about the other talented members of his family . . . He had one brother, Ifan Ellis, whose flashy dribbling on the football field could be matched only by his uncanny showmanship on the billiard table; and another brother Captain 'Boy', whose notion of 'taking a dip' was to leave his clothes somewhere near 'stage y Gwylwyr' before swimming in a direct line towards Creigiau Mawr and beyond. Sometimes, for a change, he would strike out towards the horizon and disappear from sight for an hour or two, re-appearing as the fishing boats returned home for the night. Captain Boy's only rival as a long-distance swimmer was Glyn Pritchard, son of the Reverend Owen Pritchard who was minister of Capel Isa. Glyn, too, spent many hours at a time forging through the water like a tireless grampus. Compared with those two deep-sea mammals, the rest of us were like so many jaunty frogs in a goldfish pond.

Far and away the most articulate expert on our list was Mr John Parry 'Glandon', a big, genial man who enjoyed the reputation of rarely sending out any bills to his poorer customers, and who liked nothing better than to analyse last Sunday's sermons for the benefit of anyone who cared to listen. His personal workshop at 'Glandon' was well outside the town limits – being about half-way between Tai'r Lôn and Ddôr Ddu – but he was just as likely to be found in the local bus depot, a few yards beyond 'Siop Zebra'. We spent many hours in that draughty space, watching him build a wooden body on to a metal chassis which belonged to the Nevin and District Omnibus Company and which carried the following words clearly painted above the running-board: 'Managing Director: O. H. Parry. Maximum Speed: 12 miles per hour'.

The buses which were built in this way were square, solid, and sometimes sophisticated. At least one model had a separate 'smoking' department, placed between the driver and the other passengers, and completely sealed off from contact with the rest. It was rather like a small railway compartment, with two lateral benches facing each other, and with a door on either side.

The men who drove the buses were a distinctive breed, cheerful in a laconic way, calm, mellow, and not easily provoked by public ignorance. The three whom I remember most clearly were Messrs Thomas Jones 'Y Fron', Griffith Griffiths 'Tirgwenith', and Griffith Jones 'Cae Rhyg'. The first-named was killed while bringing home a bus-load of children from the Pwllheli County School one Friday afternoon. As the bus reached the crest of Boduan Hill, the engine stalled, the brakes failed to hold it, and it began to accelerate backwards down the steep slope. He desperately tried to stop it by reversing into a gateway on the side of the road, but the bus overturned, with fatal results. The driver died, and several of the young passengers received external or internal injuries from which some of them never fully recovered.

Mr Griffiths 'Tirgwenith' was recognised as the tortoise of the company, because he always maintained a uniform speed, whatever the circumstances, and no amount of encouragement or derision from any of his passengers would ever induce him to exceed a steady jog-trot fast enough to keep his bus on time . . .

Mr Griffith Jones had a more dashing streak in him, and (provided there were no potential spies aboard) he could sometimes be persuaded to 'step on it' along the flatter stretches, especially with the aid of a following wind. On one historic occasion, when he was in a particularly adventurous mood, he made the 7-mile trip from Nefyn to Pwllheli in 20 minutes flat, and in the process managed the unprecedented feat of travelling all the way from Bryn Cynan to Ysgol

Boduan without changing gear. The cheers which greeted this performance must have been heard in all the surrounding farms, and for a long time afterwards Griffith Jones' bus was referred to as the *Mauretania*.

Soon after the war a rival bus company was started by Mr Gawen Hughes, the local hairdresser, in conjunction (so it was said) with a Pwllheli branch of his family. It was called the Blue Bus Company, and in its early stages it consisted of one bus, with a small depot in *Stryd Llan*.

As a hairdresser, Mr Gawen Hughes was purely and simply a traditionalist, being content to run his clippers over his clients' heads until he could cut no more, merely leaving a short curtain of hair about half an inch long to droop over their foreheads. This curtain was known to the cognoscenti as a Piccadilly Fringe, and was generally considered to be less flashy than a QP. But, as a transport tycoon, Mr Gawen Hughes proved to be anything but a traditionalist. By creating this new company he threw a large stone into what had hitherto been a very placid pond, and added an excitingly fresh dimension to local life in general.

The first Blue Bus to make its appearance was sleek and shiny, with a comparatively light chassis which made the established buses look rather stodgy and cumbersome in comparison. It gave the impression that, given the chance, it could show them a clean pair of heels, and this impression was strengthened by the fact that its driver, a nephew of Mr Hughes from Liverpool, was a cheerful young man called Richie Harris who exuded confidence in everything that he did.

When the Blue Bus Company began to offer lower fares than the opposition and introduced a timetable which was elastic in practice and clearly based on the principle that the customer is always right, some of our weightier citizens expressed their disapproval of such questionable tactics, while so many others were attracted by the bait that finding a seat on the Blue Bus came to be considered something of an achievement.

Our own feelings on the issue were, to say the least, ambiguous. On the one hand we felt a certain loyalty to the old company, partly because of our family links with O. H. Parry, and partly because we respected the old adage that proven friends are best. On the other hand, the slightly piratical aura surrounding the new enterprise was not without its appeal, and at times the thrilling prospect of being on board when and if Richie Harris took it upon himself to shatter the record for the Pwllheli run was more than the most delicate scruples could withstand. Add to this the fact that, if we were lucky enough to find a seat anywhere near the driver, he might explain to us some of the intricacies of double-declutching and the other secrets of his craft.

The inter-company rivalry which throbbed steadily under the surface occasionally erupted into open competition, for, if two buses happened to leave Nefyn at about the same time, a race was inevitable, and the picking up of passengers en route became a fascinating lottery which demanded snap judgements on the part of both drivers. Sometimes, too, the long straight stretch from *Eglwys Boduan* to *Bodfel* was more like Brooklands than a country road in Lleyn, with both sets of passengers egging on their respective heroes, and the leading bus not only sticking tenaciously to the middle of the road but prepared at any moment to swerve to the right to avoid being overtaken.

Even 12 miles per hour was brisk compared with the speed of one period show-piece which sometimes trundled in from the direction of Pwllheli during the summer months, presumably for the special benefit of the visitors. This was a vintage stage-coach, drawn by two horses and complete with horn-blowing postilion, which would sweep on to the curved approach in front of the *Nanhoron Arms Hotel* and deposit its passengers there for a short stay before picking them up again for the return trip to Pwllheli. A small band of us would then set off in hot pursuit, carrying our hoops on our shoulders, trotting hard in order to keep pace with the horses, and sometimes making a special effort to jump on to the rear step. This manoeuvre was frowned upon by the driver, who showed his displeasure in unambiguous terms by swishing his long whiplash towards the back of the coach, and any boy who was unlucky enough to catch the thong on his cheek not only felt the burning pain but was likely to wear an ugly weal as a memento for the next few weeks. Despite such discouragements, we would follow the coach doggedly as far as the *Boduan Post Office*, at the point where the main road forks right for Pwllheli. There we would wave the passengers goodbye, fork left, and return home by a short cut 'over the mountain', using our hoops to encourage our rather weary legs.

Boduan was a playground for us in other ways, too. We had relatives living in *Ffarm Tyncoed*, and on fine days Robert *Dolwen* and I would walk there through the *Weirglodd*, borrow the old sheepdog Pardo, and take him to the side of the *Garn* to catch rabbits. We hardly ever caught any, because Pardo was far too old for the chase, and, as he had to jump almost vertically in order to clear the tall bracken, every leap that he took simply lengthened the distance between him and his quarry. The only rabbits which he had the slightest hope of nailing were those stupid enough to turn on their tracks and run straight at him, and even they were safe if he happened to be airborne at the time. In spite of all such frustrations, Pardo seemed to enjoy the exercise and never shirked a challenge from man or beast. When the exercise was over, it was pleasant to go down to the farmhouse and exchange the heat of the sun for the cool twilight of the kitchen, where we were given large slices of bread-and-butter and glasses of creamy milk. The slow walk back across the quiet fields with their lengthening shadows only added to our sense of well-being.

Another favourite spot was *Gors Penhyddgan*, a flat expanse of rough grass between Bryn Cynan and Boduan, on the Ceidio side of the road, where curlews and peewits nested in large numbers, and where according to Robert, precious eggs were to be had for the taking. Someone had told him that there was a ready-made market for peewits' eggs, as they were used in the manufacture of certain patent medicines, and that the local chemist, Mr Williams, was prepared to pay a handsome price for them. We never discovered the truth or otherwise of this proposition, for, although we spent many busy hours scouring the landscape, we never set eyes on a single egg. The place was so full of birds that our hopes never flagged, but they were such experienced decoys that they always managed to lead us off the scent, with the result that we invariably returned home baffled and empty-handed.

Equally popular with us were some of the neighbouring farms which, at certain periods of the year, came suddenly and vividly to life. At harvest-time we followed the *Injian Ddyrnu* from one farmyard to another, marvelling on the way at the sleek, muscular horses in their gleaming brass and leather, and then rushing away to chase mice in the grain-lofts or to play Cowboys and Indians in the open fields. At shearing-time, if we were lucky, we might be invited to join the shearers in the open-air meal which was served about noon and which sometimes consisted of delicious roast-lamb washed down with mugs of tea or buttermilk.

Our favourite event on land, however, was the Easter Monday Horse Show, the *Mownti*, which had all the attractive ingredients of an Eisteddfod without any of its hideous embarrassments. The show was usually held in *Cae John Bull*, between the 'new' church and *Caeau Capel*, and the entrance to the field was jealously guarded by Captain Wilson, who, as Treasurer of the local Agricultural Society, sat in a coach which not only served as a booking office for the day but was also intended to block the only gap in the perimeter of *Cae John Bull*.

Captain Wilson was a courteous, popular gentleman who limped painfully because he had one good leg. For many years he had served on ships of the Robert Thomas company and met with more than his share of bad luck. At the turn of the century he was Mate of the *Powys Castle* on her last voyage from Hamburg to Seattle with a cargo of cement. With such a cargo no one could afford to make mistakes, but, on approaching Cape Horn, she foundered and became a total loss somewhere between the Falklands and the Tiera del Fuego, her officers and crew having a rough time in open boats and mountainous seas before being picked up by an Argentine man-o'-war and taken to Port Stanley. Later he commanded the *Criccieth Castle* and other Robert Thomas barques until a serious accident resulted in the amputation of one of his legs and forced him to leave the sea.

When we came to know him, Captain Wilson was an Insurance Agent. He was also a keen amateur painter in water colours, and on fine summer evenings he would rig up his easel near the cliff edge, stretch out his cork leg before him, and set to work on a picture of the Bay and the Rivals, with the Anglesey coastline lying flat and low on the horizon. If we happened to come by, we were welcome to stop and to talk to him while the picture slowly grew and took shape. He showed a lively interest in us, asking us questions about our progress in school and about our plans for the future. We therefore had every reason to regard him as a friend. Nevertheless, as each Easter Monday approached, he became by definition an enemy. Simply by occupying that official and officious coach, he would assume, so to speak, the mantle of a Sheriff of Nottingham, challenged by bands of young Robin Hoods who would stop at nothing to escape his eagle eye for one split second so that they could slide unobserved under the main axle and emerge triumphantly, and anonymously, on the other side. The prospect of thwarting officialdom in this way added to the general sense of occasion, which began to affect us as early as the previous Saturday, when the various contestants from far and wide trotted into town to be housed in their temporary quarters at Tŷ Cerrig and elsewhere, the air vibrated with the neighing of horses, the mooing of cows, and the crowing of cocks, while the grooms strutted along as if they owned the place.

Those arrogant horsemen were not the only visitors to bring excitement into our lives, for every Friday evening the Madryn Hall became a cinema where Mr Hinton showed us, flickering on the screen, a whole world of fantasy peopled by such mythical characters as Bill Hart, Pearl White, Mary Pickford, Douglas Fairbanks, and Charlie Chaplin. The excitement generated by those celluloid epics was both intense and durable, and provided us with rich material for the lurid games which we played on other evenings in the darkening streets and lanes.

Had we been asked, we would probably have said that the heroes of those early films were the horses, as they moved with instinctive elegance across river-beds, sky-lines, and other features of those weird and wonderful landscapes. But their stories, too, left their mark upon us, by their simple insistence that crime never pays, that cruelty and injustice bring their inevitable retribution, and that happiness and the gifts of a quiet conscience come only to those who can think generously, act honestly, and shoot straight. This simplistic philosophy may not have had much hope of surviving long against the more cynical sophistication of adolescence, but it undeniably played a vital part in moulding our ideas.

Sometimes, usually on Thursdays, our games would be interrupted by the arrival of a small van, drawn by a white pony, which would take its place on the Groes and immediately attract every healthy child within reach. This was a mobile chip-shop from Pwllheli, one of the many portents sent to remind us that, however complacent we might be about our own mode of life, there were more highly developed forms of civilisation just over the horizon. Small wonder that the more susceptible among us could hardly wait for the day when they could 'pass the Scholarship' so that they might attend the Pwllheli County School, live in lodgings in that glittering metropolis from Monday to Friday, and thus be free to enjoy all its incredible amenities.

13

The Perils of Illiteracy

Surrounded as we were by such distractions, it is hardly surprising that our parents and teachers were sometimes haunted by the prospect of our degenerating into illiterate Philistines. Not that our sporadic reading habits can have differed much from those of other young boys with a natural preference for physical activity and the outdoor life, apart perhaps from the fact that our close links with the sea gave us a bias in favour of tales with a nautical tang. The trouble was, we spent so much time out of doors that we had precious little time left for reading in the daytime, and reading in bed proved a sterile exercise because our lungs were so full of fresh air that we fell asleep within seconds of hitting the pillows.

Some individual adults, like our Uncle Jack 'Gwenallt', did their best, in distinctive ways, to rouse us from our indifference. He was a highly intelligent man who had elected to earn his living as a builder cum coal merchant but whose heart was in the Wesleyan ministry, where his brother the Reverend Daniel Morris Griffith had already made a name for himself as a popular theologian. 'Moriah' chapel loomed high in his list of priorities, and he seemed to spend all his spare time poring over books and papers in preparation for the next weekly meeting or Sunday School. Pride of place on his shelves belonged to a handsome, light-blue set of Matthew Henry *Commentaries*, but he ranged freely over other pastures from Eben Fardd and Lewis Edwards (both 'Diwinyddol' and 'Llenyddol') to Carlyle, Ruskin, Emerson, and Oliver Wendell Holmes. At one stage he evidently reckoned that the time was ripe to introduce me to the peculiar mysteries of 'Cynghanedd', and he took the first step one evening, when, on finding that my homework consisted of reading a short account of the Battle of Bosworth, he suddenly launched himself into the passage which begins:

'Bu galed y bygylu
A'r hyrddio dewr o'r ddau du . . .'

Shortly afterwards, when we were in the bay and preparing to row round the point, he similarly startled me with:

'Weigh anchor, all you younkers!'

But even he, with all his controlled ebullience and robust intelligence, must have realised that he was tapping a sadly unresponsive well, and it was a long time before his shock tactics began to show results.

On the face of it, there was no apparent shortage of reading material at our disposal. In addition to the boxfuls of County Library books which reached the school at regular intervals throughout the year and which we dutifully queued up to borrow, there was also a small lending library within easy reach. This was at No. 1 Marine Terrace, where the two Miss Jones sisters (Miss Maggie and Miss Jane) had inherited a fair nucleus of volumes from former lodgers, had added to it over the years, and welcomed everyone who seemed inclined to show the slightest interest in it.

Whenever we knocked at the door of No. 1 Marine Terrace, we were greeted with a friendly smile, ushered inside the door, and proudly invited to choose from shelves packed with names like Goldsmith, Leigh Hunt, Sheridan, and Thomas Hardy. Unfortunately, the range of choice which both they and the County Library had to offer fell woefully short of our expectation, for the simple reason that on the subject of what constituted 'a good read' we rarely saw eye to eye with our elders.

They took the view that what we needed was a suitably solid diet, and that the sooner we started upon such a diet the better. The first school prize that I ever collected, at the age of seven in the Infants' department, was a well-bound, closely-printed copy of *Caban f'Ewyrth Twm*, a faithful translation of Harriet Beecher Stowe's classic. The simple illustrations were surprisingly moving and won my heart so completely that I can still see Eliza, with her baby in her arms, making her desperate dash for freedom across the ice-floes of the Ohio River. The text, sad to say, was quite unreadable.

We were no more attracted by the fare provided for us at home, where Mother saw to it that we gnawed our way steadily through such admirable periodicals as *Dysgedydd y Plant* and *Cymru'r Plant*, but could not prevent us from remaining blind to their special virtues. What prevented *Y Winllan* from being equally unappetising was the appearance of Tegla's *Nedw* and *Hunangofiant Tomi*. Our official menu also included tales like *Madam Wen* and *Ifor Owain*, and missionary publications like *John Williams, Saer Llongau* or *Livingstone y Llwybrydd* – heroic epics, in all conscience, but narrated with a somewhat unctuous zeal which drained them of their natural colour and presented their heroes as rather vapid prigs with whom we found it impossible to sympathise, let alone identify.

Far more to our taste were the various comics which appeared each week hot from the press, and, on the rare occasions when we had two pennies to spare, our first impulse was to make a bee-line for Siop Old Post to buy one of the plump little paperbacks which lay invitingly on Mr

William Jones' counter, so that we could devour the latest version of the exploits of Captain Kidd and his disreputable cronies on the Spanish Main. We knew the names of his officers and crew by heart, and talked of them as though they were close acquaintances, as in a sense they were. We also derived a deep primitive satisfaction from the knowledge that, however intricate the plot of the narrative might be, at the end of each story rough justice would be done, and virtue would triumph over all dangers and vicissitudes. Those naive, rollicking yarns, with their smoking cannon, boarding parties, flashing cutlasses, and the rest of the paraphernalia which helped to create an atmosphere of constant suspense and imminent menace, were hardly what our mentors would have prescribed, but we found them exhilarating and enthralling.

Occasionally, on birthdays or at Christmas time, Father might send us, or some enlightened friend or relative would give us, a book which proved equally satisfying, and as time went by our reading became more and more eclectic. So Mark Twain, for instance, clasped hands across the ocean with the Reverend Tegla Davies, when Tom Sawyer and Huckleberry Finn joined Tomi and Nedw in our gallery of literary heroes. Sometimes manna fell down from heaven in the most unlikely spots. Once, in Bristol, while Father visited some shipping agents in a large office block, and I sat waiting for him in the central lobby, a kind young man emerged from the agents' office and handed me a fat green volume called *Tales of Adventure*, which was packed tight with full-length stories by R. M. Ballantyne, Mayne Reid, Jules Verne, and Fenimore Cooper. I started with *The Pathfinder*, was immediately swept off my feet, and long before Father returned I had paddled miles upstream and penetrated deep into Indian territory on the first stages of an addiction which was to last for many years. When the kind young man reappeared and saw how enthralled I was, he smilingly insisted on my keeping the book, which still exists as a battered but cherished relic. As it performed the miracle of combining thrills and respectability to a degree which satisfied both my parents and myself, I was permitted to read it almost without restraint, and for that reason alone it must occupy a special place in my affections.

'Almost without restraint' means that I was not allowed to read it on Sundays, when Mother's censorship assumed tyrannical proportions. She herself appeared to derive much joy on Sundays from becoming absorbed in such special papers as *Y Tyst*, whose front page carried a London letter with the intriguing title of *Hyn a'r Llall o Babilon Fawr*, or the *British Weekly* where the contributors had unusual names like Robertson Nichol, Dr Jowett, and Joseph Hocking. Since we were expected to follow her example, it was tacitly understood that on Sundays we should confine ourselves to books with a religious or strongly moral bias. This meant in practice that our Sunday choice was restricted almost to vanishing point, and our attempts to comply with Mother's wishes placed us on the horns of a painfully recurring dilemma, for it was rarely possible to maintain for long the pretence of reading a book which we could not enjoy.

In God's good time, our dilemma was largely resolved through the good offices of Sir Arthur Mee. It is doubtful whether the benefits which that tireless writer conferred upon the children of his day have ever been adequately appreciated, for, as a brilliant populariser he surely deserves to rank with men like Syr Owen M. Edwards. Shortly after the First World War he produced the *Children's Newspaper*, which came out every week and provided material – in the shape of news items, maps, games, puzzles, serials by authors like T. C. Bridges, comments on current affairs throughout the world – broad enough in its appeal to interest any boy or girl who could read. But it was as editor of the *Children's Encyclopaedia*, with its eight sturdy volumes, that he performed his greatest service, for the *Encyclopaedia* contained sections on practically every topic under the sun, from the hammering of nails to the problems of metaphysics, and thus provided a much-needed lifeline for readers like my brother and myself. Simply because the eight volumes had a wide selection of Bible stories and of other items guaranteed to improve our minds, Mother accepted them as a legitimate part of our Sunday browsing, and in taking advantage of this dispensation we made two interesting discoveries. The first was that the Bible stories as told by Arthur Mee were more interesting than we had suspected; the second was that, after reading a Bible story, we only had to turn a page or two to find ourselves in quite different company, perhaps sharing Drake's excitement as he caught his first glimpse of the Pacific, swaggering our way with John Hawkins across the Isthumus of Panama, or on the decks of HMS Revenge 'at Flores in the Azores', helping Sir Richard Grenville to defy impossible odds as the imperial galleons of Spain lumbered into the attack and prepared to blast us out of the water. In other words, we had found the secret of moving in one short stride, so to speak, from the world of John the Baptist to that of Captain Kidd, and of thus enjoying the best of both worlds. It was a blissful revelation, for, in practical terms, it provided us with a ready-made, fool-proof means of remaining cheerfully occupied on the wettest or holiest of days. It would be an exaggeration to suggest that Arthur Mee preserved our sanity, as I doubt whether that was ever in serious danger, but he certainly helped us over an awkward hurdle, removed a growing sense of frustration, and positively enriched our young minds by opening doors and windows for us in all directions. He also served as a unique guide to other books by providing us with fascinating extracts from many classics and by making us familiar with the names and lives of great writers from many lands. Without our realising it, he whetted our appetite.

Similarly without realising it, we were further helped by the fact that both our parents read extensively and had filled many corners of the house with books. Not that we found these in any sense alluring. The first present that Mother received from Father was a handsome copy of Robert Burns' poems bought in Glasgow in 1903, and similar presents had followed it in a steady stream over the years from various parts of the world. Father himself, like so many blue-water sailors faced with long voyages, was an avid reader, his favourite authors being Daniel Owen, Scott, and Dickens. He rarely read poetry, but had a taste for Browning, whereas Mother preferred Wordsworth. Dotted about the shelves of our 'parlwr cefn' and elsewhere were volumes given to Father in foreign ports, prominent among them being a set of the *Waverley Novels* presented to 'Señor Davies' by a group of anonymous 'amigi' in Lima on 'Mai 25, '92'. Similarly on view were ranks of best-sellers by Conan Doyle, Hall Caine, Rider Haggard, Marie Corelli, Mrs Humphrey Wood, and a host of other writers whose names are now forgotten.

Some were, if only superficially, rather more intriguing than others. We occasionally looked at an English/Spanish version of the New Testament given 'To Mrs Davis, from Mrs Staff Capt. Thomas, Callao, Peru, 16.11.11'. A much larger book, written by Harry Lindsay, with a preface by the Rev. Hugh Price Hughes, had the perplexing title of *Methodist Idylls*, and a fly-leaf bearing the inscription: 'To Captain Davies, in memory of the kindness of a Welshman to me', with the signature 'C. K. Dart of Enfield NSW, 24

May 1906'. It had an equally mystifying companion called *More Methodist Idylls*, inscribed 'To Mrs Davies, Gwydir Castle, in memory of a Welshman's kindness to my husband', signed 'Maud A. T. Dart'. The wording of those two inscriptions raises questions which it never occurred to us to ask, partly because we had more immediate matters to attend to, partly for the simple reason that at that time none of those books excited in us more than a slight passing interest. In fact, the only book which exhaled any whiff of real excitement was a heavy volume issued by the Admiralty for the guidance of Merchant Navy officers in wartime, its pages filled with silhouettes of enemy submarines and surface raiders. The pictures were interesting enough, but even more so was the fact that the book covers were weighted with lead, so that, in an emergency, it could be safely dropped overboard.

That book was an exception, and we considered all the others, in contrast, to be very dull indeed. How wrong we were, we discovered by accident one day. Among Mother's favourites were several by a certain Joseph Hocking who figured also among the stalwarts of the *British Weekly* and whom we therefore dismissed from our minds as being far too edifying for our tastes. As if to lend colour to this assumption, even the books' titles – *Chariots of the Lord*, *The Coming of the King*, and others in similar vein – had Scriptural undertones which discouraged us from giving them more than a cursory glance from the outside. But one wet Sunday afternoon, when even Arthur Mee had for once failed to work his customary magic, something prompted me to take out *The Coming of the King* and to rustle its pages; and there, before my incredulous eyes, were pictures of men and women whose flowing capes, sweeping plumes, and rich swords, deployed against a background of half-timbered houses and elegant horse-drawn carriages, clearly had little direct connection with the Bible. There were even pictures of duellists and highwaymen. Thus encouraged to take a tentative bite at the first few sentences, I was amazed to find not only that this was a story about the restoration of King Charles the Second but also that it was narrated in a brisk, unpretentious style which carried me along to the end, and opened up a vista of many similar joys to come. For some years after that I became a Joseph Hocking fan, and incidentally a lay expert on the early struggles of Methodism in Cornwall, and it was my interest in that corner of Britain which led me later to Devon and R. D. Blackmore, and in turn to Wessex and Thomas Hardy. Perhaps no three English novelists can have as little in common as those three, but for quite fortuitous reasons they are closely linked together in my mind.

14

Background Activities

Our elders may have failed to exercise as much control over our reading habits as they would have wished, but they made no such mistake in supervising our more general cultural needs. The annual programme laid down for our benefit was regular, well organised, and comprehensive.

I have only hazy memories of the Brass Band and the Male Voice Choir which flourished in Nefyn before 1914, for they were both killed off by the War, and I came to know of them mainly through finding copies of old concert programmes in odd cupboards and drawers. Other institutions were more fortunate, and after the Armistice we resumed a full round of concerts, plays, 'Cymanfaoedd Canu' and 'Eisteddfodau'.

Most of my friends heartily detested the Eisteddfod because we were all too often shanghaied into competing, and, although an occasional prize of 3d or 6d was a welcome windfall, we derived no enjoyment from making what we considered to be a public exhibition of ourselves. In our estimation the Eisteddfod was a place for show-offs, and it was not until we approached adolescence that we realised what other purposes it could serve.

Once each Spring we attended the regional 'Cymanfa Ganu' at some convenient centre like Bryncroes or Llithfaen or Pwllheli. Bryncroes had little to offer beyond the village shop, which was always jammed with eager customers, and the open fields protected by thick hedges which we dared not climb in our Sunday best. There was hardly enough time between the services to venture as far as Rhiw, with its breathtaking prospect of Hell's Mouth and Cardigan Bay . . .

In Llithfaen the main recreation open to us was to stroll sedately on the lower slopes of the Eifl. If it were less than sedately, we might come down to chapel with bilberry stains on our clothes. Only for the more enterprising among us was there the possibility of a quick jaunt down to Nant Gwrtheyrn or up to Tre'r Ceiri.

What made Bryncroes and Llithfaen so attractive was the fact that the journey there and back was sheer bliss from beginning to end. We sometimes travelled in a number of long horsedrawn 'brakes', which was an adventure in itself; and if Father or any of his friends happened to be on leave at the time, they accompanied us on these excursions, adding a thick layer of gilt to the gingerbread by plying us with fruits and slabs of chocolate. At the foot of every hill (and there were many) the men and boys dismounted in order to lighten the load, and, as we trudged up the hill and chatted gaily with our elders, we had the feeling that we were well and truly on our way towards man's estate.

When we happened to travel by bus, the same logistic problems did not arise, but it was some compensation to be allowed to make the trip on the bus roof, normally reserved for heavy luggage, with a low protective rail running round it. It also carried a huge sheet of canvas which flapped like a mains'l in the wind and was large enough to cover the luggage and the entire roof in wet weather. As we moved through the country lanes, the bus roof became a wonderful playground, for we often passed under trees whose branches were low enough for the more intrepid members of our party to swing like monkeys from one end of the bus to the other, and the generous spread of canvas enabled us to add continually to our range of improvised games. By the time we climbed down the ladder at the end of such a journey, most of us showed sad signs of wear and tear and had to be groomed afresh before being passed fit for public display.

The conductor at most of the cymanfaoedd in my time was a tall young schoolmaster from Rhiw called Mr R. H. Gruffydd, who came of a versatile Anglesey family. In those days he was a popular character in Lleyn, and to my young eyes he seemed an imposing figure as he stood erect in the pulpit, addressed the huge congregation with evident authority, and, with a wave of his baton, persuaded them to produce wave after wave of sweet harmony. He later moved from Rhiw to Penfforddelen, and many years elapsed before I had the pleasure of meeting him on level terms, but, in the winter of 1955-56, whilst preparations were being made for the Urdd Eisteddfod to come to Caernarfon, he and I worked closely together on the Pwyllgor Llên. By then he had given up both teaching and conducting, and was more widely known as an *englynwr*.

Compared with the simple charms of Bryncroes and Llithfaen, Pwllheli was like a modern Babylon or a page out of the *Arabian Nights*. It had no hanging gardens, but it did have a large model of a sheep hanging outside *Siop Pwlldefaid*; and its station, market square, town hall, and busy streets gave it the rich exuberance of a metropolis. As we walked from one shop window to the next, our feelings were a mixture of envy and awe. But our delight was not wholly unalloyed, for some of the local bravos looked upon us as fair game and roamed the streets after tea in search of country cousins whom they could safely provoke or intimidate. Their stock method was to obstruct us by standing in the middle of the pavement, sneering at our Sunday clothes, and asking superciliously; 'Noci di fi, lad?' The Sunday clothes were usually a sufficient answer in themselves, for on such a day it would have taken a rash boy to face his mother with clear evidence of having been in the wars. Gambolling on a bus roof was bad enough; brawling on the streets of Pwllheli would have put us beyond the pale.

Almost as enjoyable as the *Gymanfa Ganu* were the plays and concerts which were staged at regular intervals during each year. Most of the plays were reliable tear-jerkers like *Y Ferch o Gefn Ydfa* or adaptations of Daniel Owen which proved widely popular and attracted large responsive audiences to the Madryn Hall. Not the least responsive spectator was myself, especially if some members of the family happened to be involved in the action. One memorable performance was that in which my Aunt Miriam took the part of Mari Lewis, and Davy Richard played Wil Bryan, the pathos being so heavily underlined that towards the end my face was damp with tears and the stage had become a blur.

The concerts occurred oftener because they entailed less intensive preparation and there was no shortage of amateur talent in the area. Each chapel took it in turn to produce a Christmas entertainment and was expected to rely exclusively on home-grown performers, which meant that we were obliged to do our bit by taking part in action songs or by playing in sketches which ranged from solemn Nativity scenes to burlesque gymnastic sessions. We enjoyed the fun, but the fancy dress which we sometimes had to wear made us squirm with revulsion. At other times the organisers were free to throw their net much further and arrange to entertain us with singers and elocutionists drawn from other parts of Lleyn and Eifionydd – or even beyond! We had mixed feelings about the elocutionists, who took far too long to rant and posture and grimace their way through pieces like *Y Gloch Dân* which were supposed to be dramatic but which we found intermittently hilarious, with the result that we were constantly rebuked by our parents and other indignant elders for sniggering in the wrong places. But we relished the singing, especially if the choir and the individual vocalists came from Llithfaen.

Llithfaen had for many years enjoyed the reputation of being a nursery for singers who were blessed not only with good voices but also with a highly developed musical sense. Taid always insisted that this was due to the work done by the village schoolmaster Mr Griffith, whose ruling passion was music and who taught generations of children to read Tonic Sol-ffa and Old Notation without apparent effort. Whenever the Town Crier tramped from street to street to announce that the Llithfaen contingent were to appear in the next *Cyngerdd Mawreddog*, we knew that we could look forward to a treat, and we were never disappointed. Among the soloists, our two favourites were the tenor Hugh Evan Roberts (better known in later years as Tenorydd yr Eifl) and the bass Owen Owen (who presumably had no bardic title). We enjoyed them most of all when they came on together to sing duets, for they presented, both to the ear and to the eye, a perfect contrast. Hugh Evan was not given to extravagant gestures, but he was strikingly alert and volatile, the look on his face reflecting the changing moods which he wished to convey, and his body moving gently to the rhythm of the song. Owen Owen, on the other hand, was as solid as a rock, and his face remained impassive as his deep booming voice provided the framework on which his partner wove his elegant arabesques. The two were probably at their best in singing patriotic songs, and to hear the one thumping and the other rollicking his way through such pieces as *Y Ddau Arwr* was an experience calculated to stir the blood.

The annual round of entertainments would not have been complete without the Visitors' Concert in August. One of the most agreeable aspects of life in those days was the friendly relationship existing between us and the English visitors who invaded the place during the summer months. Many of them were cotton people from Lancashire and

Cheshire who arrived among us every year and stayed with the same families, usually throughout the month of August. Some of them had been coming to Nefyn for more than one generation, and such names as Glyn Jones, Spencer, Thompson, Richards, Higson, &c were as familiar to us as those of our next-door neighbours. Over the years we and their children became good friends and spent much time together. As one would expect, their main hobbies were swimming, sailing, fishing, and golf, but they also took an interest in the general life of the village, and, whenever any function was arranged for their benefit, they gave it their unstinted support. They helped to run the regatta, the carnival, and the sports, and contributed most of the prize money. They were equally enthusiastic in welcoming the notion of having a Visitors' Concert.

In its early stages, soon after the war, this proved to be a largely homespun affair, with local stalwarts together with volunteers from among the visitors' families venturing on to the stage with voices which might have passed muster in a private drawing-room but which tended to be lost among the rafters of the Madryn Hall. There could never be much of a future for a function where the highlight of the evening was usually Johnnie 'Glandwr's' spirited rendering of *The Old Man of Borneo*. Such a diet was bound to pall after a while, and, since good will can never be a permanent substitute for good performance, it was just as well that the Visitors' Concert was rescued from imminent disaster by Mrs Henry Williams, wife of the local vicar, who was herself a concert pianist and counted singers like Owen Bryngwyn among her close personal friends. She used her influence to persuade him and others to add substance to our annual festivities, and his popularity with his largely English audiences soon became proverbial. Having once heard him, they politely but firmly insisted on his being invited every year, and he never refused the invitation, which came to be recognised on both sides as a regular fixture. On the night of the concert, as soon as his name was announced, the applause was deafening; when he appeared, it threatened to raise the roof; and everyone listened in rapt silence as he sang his way through a series of Welsh folk-songs like *Mae gen i dipyn o dŷ bach twt*, *Dafydd y Garreg Wen*, and so on. They waited expectantly for the climax of the evening, which was his own special version of *Hela'r Sgwarnog* in both Welsh and English; and, after he had galloped his way through it at break-neck speed, they would roar their delight and clamour for an Encore, which he invariably granted, time and time again, until he had run out of breath and had to insist laughingly that he could do no more.

15

School and Chapel

Between 1914 and 1918 the boys of my age had left the Infants' Department of the local school and worked our way through the classes of the Senior School as far as Standard 6. Adjusting ourselves to the changes involved in this pilgrimage was no doubt a salutary experience for us. It was also abrasive, and at times painful, for, after two years of Miss Ellis's rather capricious maternalism, it was far from easy to come to terms with the more ruthless and impersonal discipline which was to regulate our lives for the next 4 or 5 years.

The new regime to which we had to become accustomed at the age of 7 had the virtue of being firm and consistent. We did not much care for it and often had sore hands to prove how effectively it was administered, but there was never much point in complaining about it, either to our parents or to any other adult, since the school was only playing its part in safeguarding the values and standards which they approved and which they were therefore determined to preserve.

What those standards were was no secret, for, although our parents could be remarkably tolerant, and our relations with them were warm and direct, there were some matters on which they brooked no argument. Like so many of their contemporaries in other parts of the country, they were clear in their own minds about the difference between right and wrong, between good and bad, between courtesy and boorishness, between the acceptable and the forbidden. Nowadays such terms may be dismissed as unduly emotive, but our parents never hesitated to use them as a basis for making moral judgement or for asserting their authority. As they saw things, the code which they followed had long proved its validity in practice, a fact which automatically placed them under a moral obligation to transmit that code to us, whether we liked it or not. And their right to do so was founded on their belief that, if the best school of all is Experience, it follows that the old may reasonably be expected to know more than the young. 'Yr hen a ŵyr, a'r ifanc a dybia'. They had no time for the over-confident upstart who teaches his grandmother to suck eggs, or, as they put it, 'yr oen yn dysgu i'r ddafad bori'. In their eyes, precociousness was unnatural and therefore to be discouraged.

Whatever one may think of the logic of their reasoning (and I, for one, have no quarrel with it), no one can doubt the integrity of their intentions, since, in extolling such virtues as courtesy, unselfishness, subordination and 'good manners' generally, they were simply hoping to ensure a better world by inducing in us a form of self-discipline which might give the gentler and more constructive parts of our nature a chance to survive and to assert themselves against their more destructive counterparts. What is even more to their credit, they had the wit to realise that such a creed worked both ways, in the sense that, while it called upon the young to be properly humble and responsive, it no less clearly called upon the old to be correspondingly sympathetic and responsible. In other words, although we were held on a tight rein, the hands which held the reins were never harsh. There is no doubt in my mind that we were lucky to spend our formative years in a society which, whatever its limitations, at least knew its own mind and had the courage to declare it, for the net result was that we enjoyed the inestimable advantage of knowing precisely where we stood and what was expected of us. Frustrated we may have been from time to time, but we were never confused.

In other words, there were axiomatic truths or basic principles which formed, so to speak, a boundary fence beyond which we strayed at our peril. We were constantly made aware of this barrier, wherever we might happen to be. Even when we played out on the streets, if our conduct or language departed noticeably from the expected norm, adult passers-by were likely to pause and admonish us, some more tartly than others. But nowhere were those basic truths more consistently and emphatically drilled into us than in the village school. Within those thick grey walls, which were officially condemned over half a century ago but still stand intact in all their massive strength, we were taken in hand by a team of teachers who, in both temperament and appearance, represented a wide diversity of types, but who all worked as a team to achieve one common aim, which was to lick us into shape.

They included lively characters like Miss A. B. Jones, who once penalised me so heavily for daring to use the expression 'a lot of . . .' that I have avoided it like the plague ever since . . . Miss Evans, a native of Anglesey who, whenever she became over-wrought (which was often), amused the boys and embarrassed the girls by threatening us in certain words which clearly showed that they did not mean the same to her as they did to us . . . Mr Bert White, a native of Pwllheli who survived the worst years of the War, who habitually rode to school on a motorbike, and who, before he was killed in a road accident near Penprys, endeared himself to everyone by his natural geniality and by his capacity to make jokes even in Arithmetic lessons . . . Mr John Jarrett Parry, who died of consumption at a comparatively early age, and who, during his brief spell on the staff, began to open my eyes to the magic of poetry and had the temerity to introduce us to passages from 'A Midsummer Night's Dream' . . . And Mr James Cook, who was so short sighted that he never managed to catch the boys guilty of curtailing some of his afternoon lessons by surreptitiously moving forward the hands of the classroom clock, and whose glasses were so thick that it was a great joy to find him bending over our books, so that we could peer sideways and catch glimpses of an unbelievably tiny world.

The undisputed leader of this team was Mr Owen Williams, a native of Felinheli and a product of the Bangor Normal College. A short, round, dapper man with a neat moustache. Mr Williams had come to Nefyn at an early stage in his career, recognised a good thing when he saw it, and stayed there for the rest of his life. He made it known to every generation of children which passed through the school that his personal motto was 'Thorough', and he never deviated from that idea. There were many times when we wished that he would. We welcomed the rare mornings when he came into Prayers wearing a signet ring, for this usually meant that he would be off for the day, perhaps to attend a meeting of the Education Committee or to fulfil some other official duty, for he was a man of many parts. Before the First World War he had trained and conducted a highly successful Male Voice Choir in the area; for many years he served as Secretary of 'Soar' Congregational Chapel and as Hon. Sec. of the Nevin & District Golf Club; bringing to all these activities the same persistent application and untiring sense of duty. It came as no surprise to those who knew him that one of his heroes was the loyal but ill-fated Earl of Wentworth, a copy of whose portrait hung on the wall of Standard Six.

In short, Mr Owen Williams was a spartan disciplinarian whose word was never questioned either inside or outside the school, and whose influence over his pupils persisted long after they had reached maturity. It was an object lesson to watch him stand on the stage of the Madryn Hall during a Saturday night concert, when a few unruly elements threatened to disrupt the proceedings, and, by simply pointing his sharp index finger in the direction of the culprits, reduce them instantly to abject silence. His own self-control appeared to be absolute. When his wife and only son died in the flu epidemic of 1919, he revealed no sign of the grief which he must have felt. Although he could be moved to anger, we never once heard him raise his voice. On the other hand, we never once heard him laugh. I doubt if we ever saw him smile, as he seemed to have no time for such levity. This apparent coldness meant that we were never allowed close enough to develop any real affection for him, and the fear which he engendered in us in school remained as a permanent barrier between us. Even so, we respected him, for we felt, even in our early days, that he was in earnest, and that, in his austere unbending way, he did his duty as he saw it. Along with parents and countless others he performed the invaluable task of providing us with clear guide lines which were intended not as a strait-jacket to restrict and impede but rather as a support for us to grasp and to lean upon in the testing days ahead. For that service they deserve our undying gratitude.

The fear which Mr Owen Williams evoked in us never degenerated into panic or aroused any deep resentment. The reason, I suspect, is that in time we became so conversant with the rules of the game that we learned what pitfalls to avoid, and, when we were unlucky enough to be caught committing an indictable offence, we accepted the consequences as a necessary evil. They were not welcome, but at least they were predictable, and in this sense did not outrage our elementary sense of justice or knock us morally off balance.

Our relations with Mr Davies the School Attendance Officer came into a different category. Whenever he came through the door, the mere sight of him made our nerve-ends tingle; we would begin to rake frantically through the ashes of our recent behaviour and shudder at the prospect of what we might find. For his arrival meant that one of us might be deemed worthy of a berth on *HMS Clio*, a convict-ship (so we thought) which was moored in the Menai Straits and served as a place of torment for those boys whose school attendances or behaviour fell below par. In later years we were to discover that Mr Davies was a pleasant and even cheerful gentleman, but that discovery could never efface the memory of the crippling panic which his visits induced.

* * *

The discipline so rigorously enforced by the school was steadily reinforced by the chapels. As chapel members, our parents regularly attended three services on Sundays and at least two during the week, and, almost as soon as we could walk, we were gently but firmly taken in tow. In the earliest stages, when we were still too young to have strong personal views on the matter, the practice cannot have seemed as unwelcome as it later became, for I have memories of many a cosy hour spent in our box-like family pew, especially on dark evenings, when we snuggled up against our older companions, listened to the surge of singing which swept over us at intervals, watched the flames flicker in the brass lamps located at strategic points along the aisles and on each side of the pulpit, admired the coloured patterns on the ceiling and on the high arch behind the preacher, marvelled at the large bearded men who sat with Taid in the *Sêt Fawr*, wondered how on earth Mother and the other ladies present could possibly push their hat-pins through their heads, and generally wallowed in a half-curious, half-drowsy state of well-being. The distinctive smell evoked by such memories is a subtle blend of furniture polish and Eau de Cologne (or Florida Water).

As we grew up and became more detached, I doubt whether we would have continued the practice of our own free will, but the simple fact is that we were given no choice. We were fitted willy-nilly into the accepted scheme of things, and on the whole it must be said that we acquiesced with tolerably good grace, for any protest would have been, at worst, a grave offence, and, at best, a waste of time.

It was easier to acquiesce on Sundays than on weekdays, since all our friends were then subject to similar regimentation and village life generally revolved around the chapels. Moreover, the hardships of compulsory attendance could be alleviated in various ways. E.g. each of my aunts who shared our pew carried a muff from which a sweet or two might emerge at the psychological moment; and if I were lucky enough to be pushed into the far corner, there in the pew on our right sat Mrs Jones 'Cynlas', who could always be depended upon to keep us alert with a steady flow of gelatines. These formed her staple diet on Sunday evenings, and she would sometimes whisper to me on the way into chapel, 'Fydd Mr . . . ddim yn hir fel arfer. Rhyw bum neu chwe gelatine ddylai neud y tro. Gawn ni weld'.[14]

On the whole, the sermons formed the most trying part of the service for my brother and myself, and in our younger days we were naturally more concerned about their length than their content. Since we had no watch of our own and dared not turn back to look at the clock, we had to rely for clues upon the man in the pulpit. The type of preacher whom we considered most helpful was the one who left his Bible open after giving out his text, and some 30 or 40 minutes later closed it purposefully as he approached the end of the line. With him we knew just what to expect, and, providentially, most of our visitors came within that humane category . . . A type who annoyed us intensely was the one who closed the Bible immediately after reading the text, thus leaving us with no hint whatsoever as to when the end would come. But worst of all was the sadist who kept his Bible open most of the time, closed it ostentatiously after about half an hour and so deluded us into believing that it would soon be over, only to re-open it afresh and set out on a second peroration which seemed interminable. Such cat-and-mouse tactics made a mockery of the religion which the man affected to preach.

Perhaps the oddest preacher of all in our opinion was a man from Llangwnnadl called Bodvan Annwyl, who differed in almost every respect from every other preacher in our experience. Throughout the service he stood as still and upright as a ramrod, conveyed the impression that the singing of hymns was a ritual which he perforce accepted but could not approve, and spoke in a flat, monotonous voice which, if you shut your eyes, sounded as though it came from a distant cave. Mother and Taid both insisted that he was worth listening to, although they conceded that most of what he had to offer might be a bit above our heads. In our view, his most interesting feature, apart from his name, was the deafness that compelled him to wear a hearing-aid attached to a battery which he placed on the pulpit lectern and which at regular intervals crackled like a bonfire. But for such distractions, his sermons would have been insufferably dull.

As we grew older, we began to fidget less, and to listen more, fitfully at first, but by no means fruitlessly, for most of the preachers whom we heard were such masters of their craft that they were capable of catching us unawares, so that, given time, something was bound to stick. Occasionally they had engrossing stories to tell, now and then a vivid illustration would light up the service even for a ten-year-old, perhaps a name or a passing observation might rivet our attention and momentarily make us tick. We even began to discriminate between them and to have our favourites – men like the Reverend William Jones, Nant Ffrancon (also known as Mr Jones *Mountain Ash*), who so often illustrated his text with simple parables couched in language well within our reach. Though I cannot recall his actual words, I can still hear him describing a neck-and-neck marathon race between Faith, Hope, and Charity. At what stage we ceased to be unwilling spectators and became listeners it is impossible to say, but a few isolated incidents stand out like tiny milestones in the memory. E.g. when Dr Miall Edwards preached from the text 'Wele yr wyf yn sefyll wrth y drws ac yn curo', and explained that in Holman Hunt's famous painting there is no outer handle on the door because it can be opened only from within, he prodded me into sitting up and taking notice; and when the Reverend Gwynfryn Jones described the Magi who came to worship the new-born Christ as 'dynion yn addoli'r sêr' and added the dry comment: 'Ond mi fyddai'n well gen i blygu i seren nag i sofren', he may not have coined a particularly subtle epigram, but he at least made one small boy curious to know what on earth he meant. Most important of all, three times every Sunday we were introduced to superbly rolling, rhythmic passages from Bishop Morgan's Welsh Bible, and to some of the finest religious poems in the language – an experience bound to leave its mark sooner or later upon all those above the rank of moron. The then prevalent custom of compelling us to commit many of those passages to memory was secretly resented as an intolerable imposition, but it could not blind us to their beauty.

The weekday evenings were still more unpopular with us

for the sufficient reason that they cut drastically into our playing time, especially in the summer, when the prospect of having to leave the sunshine and some of our more fortunate comrades in order to spend a bleak hour or more in the chapel vestry cast a gloom over the rest of the day. The sense of relief when the meetings were over was indescribable.

At 7 p.m. on Monday came the *Cyfarfod Gweddi*, which occupied at least one hour during which three members took it in turn to choose a hymn before leading the congregation in prayer. One thing to be said in favour of this arrangement was that it remained reasonably uniform, and, as each prayer usually took 10 to 15 minutes, we learned from experience that, if the third participant stood up to play his part shortly before 7.45, we might fairly expect to be out on time. Only when someone proved to be abnormally eloquent were we in danger of being detained much beyond 8 o'clock. The fact that the vestry clock hung on the side wall to our left meant that we were able to time the proceedings as we went along and to regulate our feelings accordingly; and if by chance we were later called to account for letting our attention stray in that direction, we could imply (without actually lying) that our eye had been caught by the large dark-framed photograph of eminent men entitled '*Oriel yr Annibynwyr Cymraeg*', which also occupied the same wall and displayed an assortment of disembodied heads wearing beards and high starched collars, and staring resolutely to the various points of the compass.

The format of the Seiat on Thursday evening was much more flexible, no doubt an asset to the adults taking part, but for the rest of us an additional cross to bear. After the introductory lesson and prayer, which together might take up half an hour, the meeting was thrown open to any member, male or female, who had some 'profiad' to relate. Since the term 'profiad' was interpreted in the most liberal sense, there seemed no limit to the topics which might come to light in this way, and, as the meeting developed, the women were encouraged, and the children were expected, to contribute an extract from either the Bible or the hymn-book and then to answer questions about it.

If a sailor happened to be home on leave, he might have an unusual, even exciting, contribution to make. If he was asked to read the lesson, it was an odds-on chance that he would select either Psalm 107 or Chapter 27 of the Acts of the Apostles. There were no prizes for guessing what hymn he was likely to choose, . . . Sometimes, in order to avoid going too far off course, the Seiat might concentrate on one specific theme – the previous Sunday's sermons, e.g., or a recent article in the *Tyst* or *Dysgedydd* or *British Weekly*, or the significance of such terms as 'yr Iawn' or 'Cydwybod' or 'Etholedigaeth drwy Ras'[15] – but in all such cases we faced the same hazards, for some of the speakers simply did not know when to stop, and, once the wind had filled their sails, the meeting could drag on indefinitely.

Time taught us that there was, as in chapel, more than one way of relieving the tedium. For one thing, we could quietly turn over the pages of the hymnbook and stage a match between Elfed and Pantycelyn by counting the number of hymns credited to each contestant over a certain number of pages or for the duration of one of the addresses. Pantycelyn usually won hands down, although Elfed had one or two purple patches to his name, but few of those matches were ever completed as they were more than likely to be interrupted by a light prod or a heavy glance from Mother. When all else failed, we could always watch Mr William Hughes *Penybryn*. He was a short, squat, bearded ex-sailor who always looked to us as though he had just stepped out of that well-known advertisement for Skipper's Sardines. It was said that, after a somewhat irregular youth,

Mr Hughes had mended his ways overnight, when, during the Revival of 1905, he happened to roll past *Capel Soar* on his way home late at night and heard his daughter's voice praying on his behalf. The experience had sobered him in more senses than one, for he had become a regular member of *Capel Soar* and remained loyal ever since. During the winter services in the vestry he occupied a reserved seat close to the fire, seeing to it that the flames kept going by pushing bits of coal into the grate, sometimes with his bare hands, sometimes with a rather noisy pair of tongs. Like some sailors, he was an inveterate tobacco-chewer, and at odd moments the silence was broken by a sizzling sound as he spat, from varying distances but with unfailing accuracy, into the blaze.

Despite such diversions, Thursday remained for us the worst day of the week, and many years went by before we even began to conceive that there was anything to be said for those dull protracted evenings. But in time we came to suspect that they served a uniquely useful purpose, and to appreciate that the solemn disquisitions which had been the bane of our young lives were the fruit of much honest heart-searching, slow deliberate reading, and hard careful thought. Unfortunately, growing pains blinded us to the fact that we were privileged to watch a generation of unpretentious, self-taught men groping for a corner of the truth and trying to unravel some small part of the mystery of life.

In other words, the chapels in our day were not only the focal points of village life; they also proved to be for many of us a special kind of academy. With hindsight, it is clear that I was in one respect exceptionally lucky, for my father was a Wesleyan and my mother a Congregationalist, with the result that I had the best of both worlds. For one thing, I attended two Sunday Schools, Capel Wesla in the mornings and Capel Soar in the afternoons. In the latter I remained for many years in a class composed exclusively of my contemporaries, but in the former, which had fewer members, it did not take me long to gravitate to the senior class – 'Dosbarth Sêt Fawr'. This was in fact a highly specialised Debating Society where callow youngsters like myself were expected to pit their wits against men who were old enough to be our grandfathers, who could juggle effortlessly with the most abstruse theological terms, who knew every nook and cranny in the Bible like the back of their hands, and who seemed to have read every authority from 'Awstin Sant' to the Rev. Richard Jones, B.A. It is to their credit that, despite the overwhelming advantages which they enjoyed, they accepted all young members with good grace, encouraged them to speak their mind with complete freedom, and listened to them without impatience or condescension.

It did not take one long to realise that the more seasoned campaigners who formed the nucleus of the class divided naturally into two camps – 'Calvins' and 'Armins' – and that most discussions, whatever their origin, were sooner or later bound to culminate in a confrontation between the believers in Predestination and the proponents of Free Will. Sometimes these profound theological splits were to be found within one family, as in the case of the two brothers, William and Richard Thomas. The former was a tailor who spent most of his life sitting cross-legged on a table and became a convinced 'Calvin'; the latter was a quarryman who spent his days on the open rock face and became an equally convinced 'Armin'. The regular duels between these two brothers were among the highlights of many a Sunday morning, and although they were both equally intransigent in their beliefs, they remained the firmest of friends. Much of what they said went right over my head, but at least they introduced my generation to a new vocabulary which helped us to listen to the preacher in the evening service and so form some notion of what he was talking about. A stimulating experience, no doubt, but also a taxing one, and on most Sunday afternoons it was a relief to join my young friends in Capel Soar to consider matters that lay more within our province, and to wrestle with dialectical pygmies of my own size.

One of these was Wil Hughes 'Tanyfron', with whom I shared a close friendship over many years. He was about 18 months my senior, but we enjoyed the same things, and he proved to be not only one of the most unselfish and level-headed characters that I ever met but also a staunch ally in adversity. I discovered this for the first time when, on a Sunday School trip to Harlech one Whitsun, he and I detached ourselves from the crowd and went to inspect the castle. There, in one of the large empty halls we noticed that, half-way up the wall, a narrow ledge ran from one end of the hall to the other. Having first made sure that there was no one else in sight, we decided to have a shot at traversing the ledge. Since it was only a few inches wide, the only way to do so was to shuffle sideways in gingerly fashion, with our backs firmly pressed against the wall . . . Wil went first, and slowly but methodically reached his goal in safety. When it came to my turn, everything went smoothly until I committed the cardinal sin of looking down. Immediately my bones turned to water and I knew what it is to be literally paralysed by fear. I could only stand there like a statue, close my eyes, and pray that some miracle might occur to put life back in my limbs. I have no idea what would have happened if Wil had not worked his way back to my side and persuaded me to complete the journey.

Our teacher for some years in Capel Soar was Mr John Watkin Jones, whom we remembered seeing during the war as a young officer chugging here and there on his motorbike, with his R.W.F. flash fluttering behind him in the breeze. He was later to become headmaster of the Nefyn School, but in those early days, when he first took us under his wing on Sunday afternoons, he worked somewhere in Eifionydd and came home only for weekends. We took to him immediately as a personality, and surreptitiously admired the natty suits and silk ties which he wore, but we grew to admire still more the wide range of interesting information which he regularly placed at our disposal, and the apparently effortless ease with which he induced us to share his enthusiasm for the Bible and its background. His wife, Mrs Elizabeth Watkin Jones, had comparable gifts and was soon to become known throughout Wales as the author of historical tales for children.

In Capel Soar the Sunday School proved even more interesting whenever Captain Jones 'Cemlyn' happened to be home on leave. He was a miracle worker, being the only man who could and would provide us with the previous day's soccer results. His wife was English, a native of Bolton, and frequent visits to that town had made Captain Jones not only a fervid supporter of Bolton Wanderers but also a more indulgent Sabbatarian than most of his Sunday School mates.

When Bolton Wanderers won the FA Cup with revolting consistency in the early 1920s, he was the happiest man in Lleyn. My brother and I supported Cardiff City, whose progress we followed with fanatical devotion. In those pre-radio days the aficionados who could not wait until Monday morning for the results relied for earlier information upon the Football Pink, which was released in Liverpool early on Saturday evening but dawdled so much on its way across the Welsh border that it did not sneak into Nefyn until noon on Sunday. Captain Jones regularly received a copy of the Pink through his back door, and, by the time that we met outside chapel just before 2 o'clock, he was usually in a position to put us out of our agony. If for some reason we missed each other on the way in, and found it impossible to communicate in words because our classes were too far apart, he used a special code of signals for my benefit. To indicate the Bolton result, he would first of all point to himself and then hold his thumb up or down or horizontally to represent a win or a defeat or a draw. For the Cardiff City result he would point to me before moving his thumb accordingly. When the Cardiff team reached the First Division and had regular fixtures with Bolton, those matches took on a special significance, and, for anyone wishing to know the result, the look of controlled ecstasy on Captain Jones' face made any other signal superfluous. One could not help marvelling at the deft way in which he sent out his messages without being detected by his teacher, Mr John Hughes, who would have been aghast to know that one of his disciples could stoop to such folly.

John Hughes was a husky white-bearded ex-quarryman who ruled the members of his class with a rod of iron. He spent the week preparing subtle theological traps for their benefit and insisted that they read their Commentaries with due care so that they could recognise, even if they had no hope of evading, such hazards. Nothing delighted him more than to lead them up the garden path, and, whenever one of his traps was sprung, and his victims were reduced to baffled silence, John Hughes's burst of laughter would explode across the chapel like the crackling of a gorse fire.

Another advantage of being associated with two chapels was that, when I reached the sermon-tasting stage, I came to know a wide range of preachers from both denominations. Among the Wesleyans the names which figured automatically on the big occasions were Tecwyn Evans and John Roger Jones, but there were plenty of others much nearer home – Conway Pritchard, Garret Roberts, W. O. Jones (Aber), Berwyn Roberts – whom we heard regularly and who in their vastly different styles knew the secret of keeping a congregation interested and alert. No two men, for instance, could have afforded a more striking contrast than Garret Roberts with his restless histrionic gestures and Berwyn Roberts with his calm, meticulously analytical approach. For the former, a text was raw material for drama; for the latter, it was evidence to be examined under a microscope. Tegla's name does not appear on the list because until 1926 I had never seen him and thought of him only as the creator of *Nedw* and *Hunangofiant Tomi* . . .

On the Congregational side our most eminent visitors were men like W. J. Nicholson, Elfed, Pedrog, Miall Edwards, Peter Price, with a host of younger men pushing hard at their heels. One broad difference between the two sets of preachers – and it became more noticeable as time went on – was that, while the Wesleyans concentrated in general upon the moral and philosophical implications of their beliefs, the Congregationalists seemed to go a stage further and stressed some of the social obligations involved in being a Christian.

We also looked forward from time to time to hearing certain individuals in whom, for local or family reasons, we took a personal pride. Capel Wesla always reserved a special welcome for Daniel Morris Griffith, who had been brought up two doors away from the chapel, and whose tall, spare frame and ascetic face suggested a Jesuit priest rather than a 'gweinidog Wesla', and for R. W. Jones (referred to by us as 'Uncle Robat "Siop Groes" '), another high, gangling figure who came of a sea-going family and whose brother Thomas had been Master of the ill-fated *Dominion* when, sailing in ballast from Honolulu to Vancouver, she ran into a hurricane and disappeared with all hands . . . Capel Soar had a similarly warm regard for Henry Jones of Trefriw who had been born and bred in No. 1 Marine Terrace, whose two sisters still lived at the old address, and whose son Billa was later to be better known as the poet William Jones of Tremadog.

In a slightly different category was John Owen of 'Engedi', Caernarfon. As a Calvinistic Methodist, he was technically outside the pale, but in our view he more than compensated for that by being a native of Morfa Nefyn and a cousin of my father's. Consequently, whenever Father was at home and ''r hen John' happened to be preaching in Capel Isa, we considered ourselves entitled to break the family rule of 'dim crwydro ar y Sul'[16] by going there to see him. As boys, we found his sermons rather dry, but we liked the man. With his stocky frame and rock-like stance, he always looked at home in the pulpit. More than once it struck me how equally at home he would have looked on the poop of a sailing ship.

Many of these preachers also enjoyed a high reputation as popular lecturers on a surprisingly wide range of topics. They included of course men of solid substance who lectured accordingly, and were widely acclaimed among the intelligentsia. The Reverend John Owen on 'Sir Henry Jones' or the Reverend Hugh Hughes (*Braich*) on 'Billy Sunday' could always be relied upon to attract large and earnest audiences. But such a heavy diet was not for boys of my age, and, although we were forced to take some doses of it, it made little impression upon us. The only thing that I can remember about Billy Sunday is that, when he was a young boy, he ran 'like a hare'. Much more congenial were the light-hearted talks which were given in the chapels from time to time and which we eagerly flocked to hear. No Watchnight service in *Capel Wesla* was ever complete without an address by the Reverend W. O. Jones, Aber, whose robust brand of humour appealed to all ages, and who never failed to usher out the Old Year with a long salvo of funny stories which reduced us all to helpless laughter and which became part of our communal repertory of jokes for the next twelve months. After such hilarity for the best part of an hour, it was no easy task for him to call his congregation to order just before the first stroke of midnight so that he might lead us in prayer and help us to cross the threshold into the New Year in a proper spirit of devotion, but somehow or other he always managed to do it.

One of the most welcome visitors to the *Gymdeithas Lenyddol* in *Capel Soar* was Pedrog, whose post-war trip to America had provided him with a wealth of characters and incidents which he wove into an enthralling patchwork of fact and fantasy. With his long lean frame, erect bearing, and trim white beard, Pedrog had the look of a dignified, benevolent patriarch, but he also bubbled with a sense of fun and could never resist the temptation to startle his audience by suddenly giving his more conventionally interesting stories a sharp sardonic twist or a touch of the macabre. His description of a nightmare which he had one night, after missing the last train out of Buffalo, had us sitting on the edge of our seats, and made our blood run colder and colder until the unexpected ending suddenly relieved the tension and produced an audible gasp of relief from us all. For a period in the early 1920s Pedrog lived in Nefyn at the home of Captain and Mrs Davies *Plevna*, who had been members of his church in Liverpool; and he then gave us the benefit of some of his other talks, of which I best recall 'Fy Nghyfaill y Meddyg'.

---

[14] 'Mr. –is not long as a rule. About 5 or 6 gelatines should be enough for him. We shall see?'

[15] 'The Atonement' or 'Conscience' or 'Predestination by Grace'.

[16] 'no wandering on Sundays'.

16

The Beach

All those dry-land activities kept us so busy that we had little time for introspection or boredom, but, however absorbing they might be, they could not blind us to the fact they were ultimately of secondary importance in our lives. For us, the sea remained the dominant factor. Even when we temporarily turned our backs upon it and behaved as though it did not exist, it was still there, indirectly shaping our future, and to some extent colouring all our thoughts and feelings. This was not just a romantic notion but a simple fact of life.

Nefyn was never a port in the generally accepted sense of that word, and the only ships which could spend any time inshore were those which were broad-beamed and flat-bottomed enough to be able to sit comfortably on the sand between tides. This meant that, unlike our contemporaries in Caernarfon or Porthmadog, we had no extensive wharf or quayside where we could while away the hours by eavesdropping on the conversations of strange men, or by watching holds being filled or emptied, as ships of various rigs and shapes floated in and out with the tide. Since no man or child can have everything, we were denied that particular mode of contact with the outside world. Instead, we were given two well-sheltered bays completely free of treacherous currents, where boys could swim and sail without risk, and magnificent stretches of sand which served as a universal playground throughout the year and which during the summer months fairly throbbed with life and movement.

High on the list of attractions was the annual regatta held in August. This was always a stirring event. Practically every house from the *Nanhoron Arms Hotel* onwards along the Morfa road had colours flying from its flagstaff, and we could feel the excitement mounting as we ran along the cliffs after breakfast to watch the yachts jockeying for position before setting out on their wide circuit between Porthinllaen and the bar at Abermenai. Over the years, some of those yachts, like *Redwing*, became household names, for we took a professional interest in their progress throughout the summer and noted their form in other, less important races held elsewhere in Lleyn. In the afternoon, after a hurried meal, we would rush down to the beach to watch and to take part in the 'Sports', which consisted of rowing and swimming events in the bay, a variety of greasy-pole competitions and seemingly endless obstacle races on the sand. The day usually ended with a frantic free-for-all in the water between *Creigiau Bach* and *Creigiau Mawr*, when a duck was let loose from one of the boats and became a prize for any swimmer persistent enough, or lucky enough, to catch it. Sometimes the fun continued until the sun was low on the horizon, and the duck remained free to swim and quack another day.

Even without the regatta, the beach still drew us like a magnet in the summer months and kept us busy all day long. We regularly laid 'long lines' baited with lugworms, waited for the tide to ebb and flow, and then excitedly gathered what was left on the hooks after the attacks of seagulls, cormorants, and other predators. When the tides were exceptionally low, we might stagger out of bed in the small hours to scoop up sand-eels (*llymriaid*) which were easy to fry and tasted like fine whiting. We netted shrimps in the larger rock-pools as the tide ebbed around the point, and from time to time we explored the crevices of 'Creigiau

Mawr' in vain attempts to locate the crabs' and lobsters' hide-outs, for they were known only to a few, who kept their secret as though it were the Crown Jewels . . . We also offered our services to some of the men who spent their days on the beach and who, in different ways, indulged our passion for messing around in boats. They all wore the uniform navy-blue jersey and sea-boots, and, when they were not out fishing or digging for bait, were likely to be either repairing their tackle or else simply smoking and yarning on the green patch near their sheds. Some of them had such a proprietorial manner that at one stage we seriously thought them to be the owners of the beach.

They were a mixed fraternity. Among the kindliest of them was John Jones of the *John and Mary* – popularly referred to simply as 'John a Mêr' – a quiet, gentle man who had been one of Father's shipmates. Presumably on the strength of that connection, I was allowed to paddle around in one of his boats, *Lily, Felinheli, Willie*, or the diminutive *Rob Roy* which presented special problems because it was only half a boat and tended to move in circles. Sometimes, at the start of the season, when we helped John Jones to pull his boats from his shed to be stanched in the sea, we sang snatches of a homemade shanty:

'Pwl bach ar y *Wili*
A'r hen *Felinheli,*
Pwl bach ar y *Lili*
A chario'r hen *Rob Roy*.'

John Jones 'Tawelfa' also had been at sea with Father, but he was less open-hearted than 'John a Mêr', partly because he was by nature suspicious of other people, more especially small boys, and partly because he was keener than most to eke out his small personal income by hiring his boats to the visitors. The largest of those boats were two identical white models called Pipe and Iolo, and, whenever a prospective client asked his advice, his answer never varied: 'Pipe good, Iolo best'. No one ever discovered the grounds for this emphatic opinion.

In his younger days John Jones had been a deep-sea cook, and never tired of recounting episodes in which he had been involved in ports on both sides of the South American continent. Time and time again, it seemed, he had narrowly escaped death from such perils as typhoons, cholera, yellow fever, fire, and mutiny on the high seas. One of his pet stories concerned the *Western Monarch*, which was once sent to Bahia Blanca at a time when yellow fever was rampant in that port. Of the dozens of ships moored in the harbour, many had lost most, if not all, of their men as a result of the epidemic. More than half the crew of the *Western Monarch* had to be taken to hospital and died there; and an official edict was issued by the port authorities to the effect that all ships were to remain at their moorings until further notice. As this was more than the captain of the *Western Monarch* could stomach, he had a quick word with John Jones before deciding to make a run for it. Unfortunately, although he managed to get under way, he was quickly followed by a gun-boat which fired some warning shots across his bows and compelled him to return to port and to quarantine. He was lucky not to be bundled into gaol. John Jones derived great satisfaction from recounting such tales, and whenever possible, provided himself in the telling with a modest but crucial role.

On those days when he happened to be in a generous mood, he might order us to dig for his bait, and then, as a reward, let us take one of his boats from its moorings on the strict understanding that we stayed well within hail. If we so much as threatened to move out of range, his stocky figure would waddle to the water's edge, shake its fist in the air, and rant at us until we turned back for home. That was the limit of his indulgence, and there is no doubt that he relished telling us how unruly and ham-fisted we were as compared with his generation. His severest condemnation was 'Mi fydd hwnna'n angau i gwch', his warmest tribute 'Roedd o'n mynd fel *witch*'.[17]

We lost some of our dependence on John Jones 'Tawelfa' when I became friendly with Hugh Griffith 'Bodwyn', whose uncle, Captain Thomas 'Derlwyn' had a rowing dinghy called *Daisy* which was as beautifully light and well-balanced as a racing shell. On still, fine days it was no problem to take *Daisy* as far as the *Burjan* in Portinllaen, where we could spend a couple of hours rowing slowly around the rock, trailing two lines baited only with silver paper and hauling in one fat pollock after another before returning home in the late afternoon. In the evenings we made up parties for bottom-fishing (*mwyrio*), rowing out beyond the point and taking a careful bearing on two cottages between us and Garn Fadryn before dropping the anchor. We always enjoyed these outings, for, even if the fish were slow to bite, we could still admire the blaze of the setting sun as it lit up the high ground to the South East, or we could go on singing until the growing cold and hunger drove us home to supper and bed. We enjoyed ourselves all the more when we were joined by young apprentice seamen who were being given a short spell of shore leave and who had exotic tales to tell. Some of their tales would have appalled our elders, demonstrating as they did that sin as we understood it in Lleyn was still very much in its infancy as compared with the varieties which South America had to offer. We reacted to the more shocking revelations with a mixture of juvenile excitement and Non-conformist disapproval. Some of the more bizarre we dismissed as incredible.

Another boy of my age with whom I spent much time was Victor, one of the sons of O. H. Parry, proprietor of the *Nanhoron Arms Hotel*, who happened to be a relative as well as a close friend of my father's. O. H. Parry was a bluff and friendly character who habitually sported a check cloth cap, set at a slightly rakish angle. It took me some time to realise that he was somewhat deaf in one ear, but there was nothing wrong with his eyes, for in the days before (and after) such activities were banned by law, I often saw him standing in the bow of a gently gliding dinghy with a boathook in his hand, preparing to harpoon a flatfish on the sea-bed with the lethal accuracy of Deadeye Dick. He was in fact a man of many parts, and prosperous enough to be able to indulge his taste for pioneering on both land and water. A keen horseman, he had been active during the coaching days buying horses in Ireland and then breaking them in on Nefyn beach before selling them to other coachmen in Lleyn. Later, when the buses superseded the coaches, he played a leading part in forming the local Omnibus Company and became the owner of one of the first private cars in the village. Another of his 'firsts' was a handsome and powerful motor-boat called *Cygnet* which, with its bright teak, varnish, brass rails, and cosy little cabin stocked with soft drinks which bubbled up the nostrils, seemed like a floating paradise. To be welcomed on board and to be freely granted a share of such luxuries was both incredible and exciting, and I relished every minute of it. When there was no room for Victor and myself on board *Cygnet*, it was great fun to be towed behind its square stern, with the bow of our dinghy or small Norwegian *pram* jutting high in the air, watching the broad wake go by while the propeller churned the intervening stretch of water into a seething mixture of green and white. Yet, however thrilling the sheer speed of such a boat could be, it lacked the simple majesty of moving under sail.

Another benefactor was my future uncle Owen (Robyns-Owen) who during his few months at home bought a sailing dinghy and took me under his wing from time to time. He was a generous and impulsive man, but he was also a perfectionist who did not suffer fools gladly, and he never spared my feelings when (as was all too often the case) my performance as his crew fell short of what he expected. On good days he could be entertaining company, for he was a man of frank prejudices who made no secret of the fact that his experiences in the Far East had given him ample cause to admire the Chinese and to detest the Japs. It is ironic to think that in August 1945, a quarter of a century after those peaceful fishing trips, he was to lose his life as a prisoner of war in Manila, battered to death by a Japanese guard only a few hours before the camp was liberated by U.S. Marines.

The largest shed on the beach belonged to Captain Jones *Glasmôr*, a stout, peppery but kindly man, and the owner of a yacht which we never referred to baldly by her name but always as 'Yacht *Glasmôr*'. To do otherwise would have seemed an impertinence. She had a white hull and a bright red keel; and to our young eyes, as she made her first appearance of the season on the slipway in front of her shed, and we walked like midgets under her towering stern, she looked so enormous as to be beyond our wildest dreams. It was therefore a rare privilege for me, while Father was at home after the sinking of the *Belford*, to be allowed to make several trips in her. Like most privileges, it exacted its own price, for during one of those trips, on a sharp and choppy July morning, as we tacked into a nor'westerly breeze, I discovered for the first time and last time the full horrors of sea-sickness. At the start all went well, and the fish had begun to arrive in such ravenous numbers that they were leaping at the bait before the lead had touched the water, but then came the grisly moment of truth when I had to droop myself over the gunwhale, commend my spirit to the gods of the deep, and watch the several items of my recent breakfast reappear in reverse order. Another member of the crew, Captain Williams (Uncle John *Gwynfryn*), was also sick on that day, his explanation being that he must have smoked too much too early, but I had no such excuse. Neither of us excited much sympathy.

Our happiest days arrived when Father and Captain Jones *Cemlyn* became joint owners of *Kitty*, a neat and unpretentious 12-footer which not only had a centre-board that made her easy to handle in deep and shallow water alike but proved to be the fastest sailer of her class in Nefyn. In her we went fishing for cod and mackerel beyond *Trwyn Tal*, or, in the absence of wind, simply drifted blissfully between *Penrhyn Bodeilias* and *Penrhyn Portinllaen*. A few times we used her for nutting expeditions to *Nant Gwrtheyrn*. All these activities came to an abrupt end one wild Autumn night when a nor'westerly gale hit the bay, tore *Kitty* from her moorings, and, hurling her bodily over *Creigiau Bach*, reduced her to matchwood.

---

[17] 'He'll be death to that boat' ... 'he was moving like a witch'.

17

The Sea and Seamen

As time went on, we could not fail to realise that, for the people of Lleyn, the sea was more than just a playground. Over the centuries it had become a special kind of highway, linking them with distant places, and, by making them aware of strange peoples, creatures, and customs, had given their lives an extra dimension.

In my young days, evidence of those maritime links was to be seen and heard on every hand. There was, for instance, the practice of referring to sundry individuals by coupling their name with that of some old smack or schooner with which their family was somehow connected. Typical examples were Evan Williams *Zebra*, John Williams *Cossack*, Evan Griffith *Revival*, John Jones *John & Mary*, or Griffith Jones *Pegasus*. All these men or their fathers had either owned or commanded the vessels concerned.

There was evidence for the eyes as well. Practically every kitchen and parlour contained not only the inevitable model ship in a bottle, and colourful hearth-rugs which had been laboriously woven together to relieve the tedium of long voyages, but other exhibits like shell-encrusted frames enclosing views of foreign harbours and cities, carved ornaments of wood and bone and ivory, samples of Aztec or Inca pottery, such fashionable curios as Cape Town fern, or perhaps a fine spread of emu or ostrich feathers. Many families also had parrots, cockatoos, canaries, stuffed humming-birds, or cases filled with an assortment of dead butterflies of indescribable brilliance and variety. All these things stared us in the face, as a permanent reminder that there was an exotic and exciting background to our lives.

The women too did their share of reminding. Whenever they met together, their talk was bound sooner or later to revert to their globe-trotting husbands and to the latest report on their whereabouts, more often than not somewhere between the UK and 'the West Coast'. Not until I learned some Geography did I realise that by 'the West Coast' they always meant the West Coast of South America, and the ready way in which they rattled off such names as Antafogasta, Callao, Caleto Colossa, Talcahuano, or Valparaiso should have told me that some of them at least had been in that area themselves and knew from personal experience what they were talking about and what their men might be up against. They had also picked up fragments of their husbands' vocabulary, which they used in the most natural way, occasionally addressing the men as 'Capitan', referring to the kitchen as 'the galley', ordering the children to 'vamoose', making sly allusions to 'mañana', or (if they were in playful mood) suggesting that Mr X had a nose 'like a jib-boom' or that Mrs Y sailed down the street on Sundays 'like a pinnace'.

The most effective reminder of all was the substantial number of seamen who were always on tap. Despite the large majority who were away at any given time, the residue which remained was still strong enough to make its presence felt and to give the air a salty flavour. Most of them were Master Mariners. They were to be found everywhere – collecting their paper in Siop Old Post, playing billiards or scanning the *Journal of Commerce* in either the Liberal or the Constitutional Club, chatting with their cronies on the *Groes* or strolling slowly with their wives along the cliff walk or towards the mountain, obviously enjoying a short break from constant vigilance and suspense. Some of those who were on the verge of retirement chose to take up golf, forming with the local club a special group which arranged its own competitions and was patronisingly referred to as 'the Band of Hope'. Such patronage was hardly justified, for, even if their swing was unorthodox, they knew their way home and were Extra Masters in the art of psychological warfare.

Their tough exterior belied the fact that some of them could be sentimental about the oddest things, and there were times when such sentimentality produced the most unlikely repercussions. For example, it was still remembered in my time that, way back in 1899, Captain Griffith Jones *Pegasus* had in all innocence been the means of triggering off a feud between two well-known regional bards. The trouble had started much further back, when Griffith Jones was a small boy who took great delight in visiting his grandmother Mrs Mary Williams at 'Henfelin'. In his own words: 'Arferwn yn ddyddiol fynd i dŷ fy nain yn Nefyn, a'r peth cyntaf a ddenai fy sylw oedd hen bocer fy nain, oedd bob amser wrth ochr y tân. Byddwn yn arfer cael pleser mawr gyda hwn, drwy wneud pob math o gampiau ag ef, ac fel y deuais yn dipyn o hogyn i fyned o gwmpas, enillais gyfeillion bychain fel fi fy hunan. Wedyn arferwn gasglu y plant ynghyd gan eu gorymdeithio drwy y dref gan eu harwain gyda'r pocer fel teyrnwialen ar fy ysgwydd. Bu farw fy nain a rhanwyd ei dodrefn rhwng y teulu, a'r unig beth a chwenychais i oedd yr hen bocer. Yr oeddwn erbyn hyn yn forwr a chymerais y pocer gyda mi i'r llong fel y crair gwerthfawrocaf oedd gennyf. Bu yn llongddrylliad arnaf dair gwaith, ond bob tro gofelais ddwyn yr hen bocer gyda mi yn ddiogel i'r lan, er trwy hynny beryglu fy mywyd a cholli eiddo llawer mwy gwerthfawr gan rai, ond nid gennyf fi. Y mae yr hen bocer genyf byth, yn anwyl a chysegredig'.[18]

The plot began to thicken when in 1869 Captain Griffith Jones told his story to Mr W. Edmund Williams and Mr Robert John Pryse, who were better known in bardic circles as Bangorfab and Gweirydd ap Rhys. When he invited them to write a poem on the subject 'Hen bocer fy nain', Bangorfab took up the challenge and, from his address at 3 Panton Street, Bangor, soon produced 5 verses of 8 lines each, designed to be sung to the tune 'Old Derby'. This ditty was printed in at least two 'leading Welsh newspapers' and proved a popular success.

Thirty years later, in 1899, Bangorfab, who by then was living in the Gatehouse, Llanllechid, had his attention drawn to the fact that a shamefully truncated and garbled version of his work had appeared in *Y Werin* above the name of Ap Glaslyn, who had already made his mark as a popular composer and singer, and who during the great Revival of 1905 was to gain further fame as a fiery evangelist. Not unnaturally, Bangorfab was both appalled and outraged by what he saw, and expressed his feelings in a broadsheet printed by W. Llewelyn Ellis, Heol Fawr, Pwllheli. Reprinting his own authentic version in full, he raked the plagiarist in no uncertain terms: 'Wrth gymharu y ddwy gân hon, gwelir yn amlwg nad oes ond y pedair llinell gyntaf, a saith llinell yn y penill olaf, yn eiddo i Ap Glaslyn. Gwnaed hyn er ceisio ei ffurfio yn gân wladol, drwy ysgaru lle a pherson oddiwrthi. Beth ddywed yr Ap dynwaredol hwn wrth hyn, wys?'[19] The only agreeable feature in his affray is a post-script to the broadsheet which informs its readers that by then, 1899, the old poker was safely in the hands of Mary Williams's great-grandson, Captain Griffith Jones 'Langdale'.

The sailors whom we knew naturally came in all shapes and sizes, but of the great majority of them it could be said that they fitted into a common mould and had an unmistakable prototype who may fairly be described in general terms. He was not much above average height, with a thick neck and stocky frame which in some individuals bordered on the portly. He smiled readily, and as a rule tended to be wryly amusing rather than solemn. It would be wrong to infer from this that he did not take life seriously, for in fact he was conservative in his standards (although Liberal in politics), never questioned such matters as the sanctity of marriage and family life, was formally courteous towards women, attended divine service with unfailing regularity, and generally took a serious view of his duties as husband, father, and member of society. You could be reasonably certain that he was a teetotaller, since sobriety in a ship's master was deemed a cardinal virtue. His religious views were simple in the extreme, for, although he rarely discussed such topics, his experiences afloat inclined him to be a fatalist. More accurately, perhaps, he regarded himself as being 'in God's hands'. But he was no prig, for he also saw the funny side of life, enjoyed the sound of laughter, and had an unsophisticated sense of humour which appealed to us as children. The fact that his language was as clean as a whistle made us like him all the more, for there can be few more embarrassing experiences for a growing boy than to find himself in the company, and therefore at the mercy, of an adult who swears. There may have been colourful exceptions to this rule, but I never met any. What is more, this particular form of abstinence was not confined to dry land. Several of my father's shipmates have made a point of telling me that they never heard him swear, and one at least added the comment: 'Come to think of it, very few of us did'.

One can still glean some notion of the sort of character whom this prototype represents from the photographs salvaged from old family albums and other odd corners. Pictures of individuals were less common, but when friends met abroad they usually celebrated by going to a local studio to have a group picture taken. Among the best-known studios were Godfrey's in Newcastle NSW and Hester's in Seattle. Sometimes the group consisted of 3 or 4 friends, with perhaps an inset or two to accommodate the late arrivals; sometimes it might include half a dozen or more, with the senior members of the party sitting soberly in the front row, and the rest forming a solid wall behind. Once in a while an individual figure in the group might strike a self-conscious pose by pushing his hat well back from his brow, by either brandishing or puffing aggressively at a large cigar, and by generally assuming the air of a man who is determined to impress either the natives or the folks at home, or possibly both. But such antics were exceptional. For the most part, the men convey the impression that they regard sitting in front of a camera, waiting for the dicky-bird to click, as no better or worse than any other part of the day's work, and therefore as something to be taken in their stride. They look relaxed, with a natural dignity which it is not difficult to translate into terms of natural authority, which in turn helps to explain how they managed to gain the trust and loyalty of crews who relied upon them for leadership, and sometimes for survival. There is about most of them a quality of unflappable, serene solidity.

With a few rare exceptions, they had served their apprenticeship in sail and referred affectionately to Hugh Davies the Nailer who had helped them over the first hurdles of Navigation. By the 1920s few of them had remained true to their first love, and between them and those who had succumbed to the lure of steam there existed a friendly but unmistakable rivalry which became apparent whenever they met, and the talk was then liable to crackle with references to 'wind-bags' and 'steamkettles'. We listened-in to many of their light-hearted, bantering conversations as we accompanied them on fishing trips towards Trefor or played golf with them in the evenings.

Since they were such familiar features in the local landscape, we tended to take them wholly for granted and rarely questioned them about their experiences. Even had we done so, there is no certainty that we would have elicited much response, since most of them were laconic men who considered that they were 'only doing a job' and did not choose to talk about themselves; but there is no doubt that we should have tried our luck by following up some of their references to the Roaring Forties, the Horn, Cape Hatteras, the Straits of Magellan, the Arctic Circle, or some other notorious trouble spot. Unfortunately, we did no such thing, thus allowing those unique and irreplaceable sources of information to remain untapped, and, by the time that we woke up to realise the folly of what we had done, or rather left undone, the sources were no longer there.

Despite the fact that they belonged to an older generation, their attitude towards us was not only friendly but contained an element of what I can best describe as a touch of almost divine tolerance, as though some intuitive sympathy enabled them to overlook all sins, however heinous, which sprang from the rawness or ignorance of youth. This is well illustrated by an incident in the 1920s after I had taken up golf and reached the stage where I was expected to provide myself with a fairly uniform set of clubs instead of the motley collection which had passed muster until then. One morning, when I arrived at the club-house, the main topic of conversation was that one of our members, who had recently met with a serious accident in Antwerp, had at last arrived home. This was Captain Williams 'Hafod', Edern, who, whilst returning to his ship one dark and windy night, had been struck down by a steam engine and suffered such severe damage to his left arm that it had to be amputated. Since it was clear that he was unlikely ever to play golf again, I cycled over to his home that evening and asked whether he would consider selling me his clubs. My flesh still creeps when I recall the crass insensitivity of my request, but he never batted an eyelid. Instead of slamming the door in my face, he invited me in, and, over a glass of cool lemonade, we agreed upon the details of the transaction. He then escorted me to the door and watched me ride away. I shudder to think what his unspoken thoughts may have been.

Not surprisingly, these were men whom we instinctively respected and were proud to know. At the same time, there were a few rare individuals whom we tended to look at askance, because they were supposed to have done something which would normally be frowned upon by anyone with any regard for the book of rules. For example, Captain A . . . was said to have actually keel-hauled an obstreperous member of his crew, although a modified version of the tale implied that he did no more than toss him over the stern at the end of a rope and then tow him through stormy (or was it shark-infested?) seas until his zeal had abated. Whatever the truth or otherwise of such rumours, we all knew that Captain A . . . was a hard man, and that, if he could be pretty ruthless towards others, he showed no more compunction towards himself, for one of the last things which he did, after a critical abdominal operation, was to defy his doctor's orders by leaving his sick-bed so that he could complete a certain competition before quietly returning home to die.

Captain A . . . also enjoyed the reputation of being a crack shot with a revolver, but it must be confessed that, on the one occasion when he was allowed to demonstrate his skill in public, he did not cut a highly impressive figure. The occasion was unique and infinitely pathetic, and would certainly have outraged the conscience of R.S.P.C.A. For some mysterious reason, it had been decided that a poor horse from one of the neighbouring farms should be destroyed, and the spot chosen for its execution was a small field between the farmhouse of 'Fron Olau' and the old school. The two executioners were Captain A . . . and Fred 'Cig Rhad', the plan being that Captain A . . . should first shoot the animal in its temple and so bring it down to its knees, at which point Fred would step in and despatch it with expert speed by slitting its throat with a long, thin knife brought from the slaughter-house. Before the eyes of a curious and uneasy crowd, Captain A . . . took careful aim at the target and fired, the only outcome being that the horse whinnied, shook its head and began to bleed freely from the nose. By the time that this move had been repeated three times, with a pause between each shot but with no greater success, the unease in the crowd began to simmer into open indignation, and there was a general sigh of relief when Captain Z stepped forward, abruptly snatched the revolver away from its owner, and, walking up to the victim, deliberately shot it in the temple at point-blank range. It crumpled immediately, and obligingly exposed its long neck for Fred to complete the kill. As he bent down to do so, he looked like one of Fenimore Cooper's Red Indians about to scalp an unsuspecting Paleface.

A more successful marksman was Captain B . . . , a younger man who, not without cause, fancied his chances with a rifle. Some of us had once been horrified to see him hit a basking seal in the eye at nearly 100 yards. What made his shot all the more remarkable was the fact that he was standing in a boat at the time, and the sea in Nefyn bay was choppy. There could therefore not be much doubt about his accuracy. The propriety of what he did was another matter. When he was away at sea, it was apparently his custom to amuse himself in the Doldrums by standing in the fore-peak and taking pot shots at any misguided dolphins which happened to stray within range. Although this was bad luck for the dolphins, it was no contravention of mercantile law; but there is such a thing as natural law, and on one fine day he nearly caused disaster by raking a school of whales which were quietly minding their own business, and was forced to take panic measures to avoid a collision when the whales decided to counter-attack. It was said of Captain B that his notions of discipline were so primitive and inflexible that once at least, in a South American port, when some of his men on shore-leave narrowly failed to return to the ship by the stipulated time, he deliberately ordered the gangway to be snatched away from under their noses and left them to the tender mercies of the quayside police.

How tender such mercies could be was perhaps illustrated by the strange case of Captain R, who disappeared in mysterious circumstances in a West Coast port and lost all contact with his wife and friends. According to my informants, Captain R was a lively, normal character who was unlikely to have done anything rash or irresponsible; certainly it would have been absurdly out of character for him to vanish so perfunctorily of his own free will. The commonly accepted version of this mysterious episode was that he must have run foul of the authorities by inadvertently committing some serious technical offence, and found himself unceremoniously clapped into gaol. Whenever that theory was advanced, those who had experienced the waywardness of foreign officials shrugged their shoulders and admitted that, if such was the case, then anything was possible. The last, second-hand, report brought to Nefyn was that someone, somewhere had caught a brief glimpse of Captain R working as a prisoner in a chain-gang, but that all attempts to trace him had run into an impenetrable tangle of official denials. He was never seen again, and the mystery of his disappearance was never solved.

As we grew up against this variegated background, it was only natural that we should sooner or later get the feeling that the small village we lived in was not only old and well established but also had an importance out of all proportion to its size. Had we been able to put that feeling into words, we might have said that we did not think of Nefyn as an isolated segment of humanity but rather as part of a much larger world whose limits stretched far beyond any local horizons.

The fact that so many Nefyn families had close relatives and friends dotted here and there beyond the Atlantic and under the Southern Cross naturally helped to foster this impression. Father's long letters to Mother, as well as his postcards to us, regularly mentioned some acquaintance or other whom he had run into on his travels, for several Nefyn men were serving long stints abroad as Shore Superintendents for one or other of the bigger companies like Blue Funnel or Elder Dempster. Of Father's particular friends, Captain Dan Evans of *Tynllys* and his family were in New York, and Captain John Lloyd *Moorings* was in Montevideo. Others with whom we had family ties were stationed in Buenos Aires and in Rio de Janeiro. One result of such intimate ties was that our sailors found it possible to feel at home in most corners of the globe. For the women especially this was a heart-warming thought, and more than once I heard Mother take comfort from the fact that, whenever Father was in an Australian port, there were always two or three families in the area who kept a weather eye on all his movements and who regularly laid an extra cover on their table, just in case he turned up unannounced.

Sometimes the welcome could be more formal. During the later years of his life, each time that the *Monkbarns* came to Newcastle NSW, her arrival was literally greeted with a flourish of trumpets, for the local Mayor at that time happened to be a Welshman called Mr Morgan with whom Father had become very friendly and who saw to it that the ship was welcomed by a large and noisy crowd, a brass band, and all the other appurtenances of civic pomp. The same Mayor and his associates also arranged for the ship's officers and men to be treated like long-lost brothers, with the result that their stay in harbour (before moving down the coast to load in Sydney) became a constant round of dances, bean-feasts, parties, and visits to private houses. Some of the younger men who were emotionally unattached found themselves more or less adopted by local families, corresponded regularly with local girls, and at least two of them eventually settled down in Newcastle, carving out highly successful and lucrative careers, one in the dry-cleaning business and the other in State Administration.

---

[18] 'I used to pay daily visits to my grandmother's house in Nefyn, and the first thing that caught my eye there was my grandmother's old poker, which stood by the fire. I derived great pleasure from playing with this, and, when I grew old enough to go out and play with other small boys, I would form them into a procession and lead the way, carrying the poker like a sceptre on my shoulder. When grandmother died and her belongings were divided among the family, the only thing that I wanted was the poker. By then I was a sailor, and I took the poker with me to sea as my most treasured possession. I experienced three shipwrecks, but each time I saw to it that the old poker arrived safely ashore, even though in doing so I endangered my own life and lost things which might appear more valuable in the eyes of some men but not in mine. I still have it and cherish it.'

[19] 'A comparison of the two versions shows clearly that only the first 4 lines, and 7 lines of the last verse, are the work of Ap Glaslyn. He made these changes with a view to giving his version a wider national appeal, by eliminating all personal and local references. How does the imitative Ap hope to justify himself, I wonder?'

18

Disaster and Bad News

It was gradually, of course, that we as boys came to have any real conception of the kind of life which our fathers led, and of the endless, unpredictable risks which they faced in plying their ancient craft across the oceans of the world. On the face of it, at least, they themselves conveyed the impression that a life on the ocean wave was so ordinary, not to say humdrum, that we might easily have been lulled into imagining that their voyages were no more than large-scale pleasure cruises, wholly devoid of unpleasantness and danger, but for the fact that in Nefyn itself the sea's behaviour made such illusions unlikely.

In some respects, living in Nefyn was almost like being on an island. Even when we turned away from the sea and climbed into the hills at the back of the village, we were virtually surrounded by broad vistas of deep water, extending from Caernarvon Bay to the Irish Sea; and among the landmarks which caught the eye on either side of the water there were four of particular interest. One was the cottage 'Bryngwynt' which had a special place in the affections of local sailors because they reckoned that, whenever they were outward bound from Merseyside, the last glimpse that they were likely to get of their native heath was that gleaming white spot high up among the rocks and bracken at the foot of 'Carreg Lefain'. It was said that some Nefyn captains, as they stood on the starboard tack close in, made a practice of ordering the ship's numbers to be hauled up, as a signal to their friends on shore.

Beyond the two bays, at the far side of Portinllaen, were the house and slipway where the lifeboat *Barbara Flemyng* waited to slide into the water whenever her services were required . . . Facing us on the opposite side of Caernarvon Bay lay the flat western coast of Anglesey, with two more gleaming white spots to indicate the lighthouses of Llanddwyn and South Stack; and on clear nights, as we lay in bed, their beams joined with those of the invisible Skerries to flash across our bedroom walls and ceiling.

Those restless beams were a constant reminder to us that the sea was in reality a monster of fickle moods which ranged from the bland to the homicidal, and which needed such things as light-houses and life-boats to protect men from its rages. On still days the monster could be so placid that out in the bay, even at high tide, we had only to glance over the gunwhale to see crabs walking and flatfish wriggling on the sand below; and yet, in no time at all, often without warning, it could change from a limpid window into a cauldron of flying spray and murderous grey rollers which hurled themselves against the cliffs like titanic sledgehammers.

When such storms coincided with the spring tides, their threat was all the greater, and one of our most urgent tasks at such times was first of all to help the men to see to it that all the boats were either brought ashore and put under cover or else made as snug and secure as possible, and then to set about dismantling the beach bathing-huts so that they could be hauled well out of harm's way, which meant about halfway up the cliff side. Later, when the storm had blown itself out, we used to walk along the beach in search of 'broc môr'[20] and were always likely to pick up odd life-buoys and lengths of timber which suggested that the storm had not been without its victims. The strangest victims that I ever saw were a number of pigs which had vainly tried to swim ashore from a floundering tramp, and, in their frantic efforts to remain afloat, had ripped open their throats with their pointed hooves. Although the pig is not normally regarded as an endearing animal, there was something irresistibly pathetic about the sight of those mutilated bodies.

We could therefore claim perhaps to be not wholly unaware of the uncertainty attached to the occupation which our fathers and their friends had chosen to follow; but, as is the way with adolescents, we were for most of the time so intent on enjoying our own lives and on disentangling our own pressing problems that all such thoughts receded well into the back of our minds. Only when something out of the ordinary happened were we momentarily shaken out of our composure.

Since we had no radio in those days, we relied for information upon letters and cables, or upon Board of Trade reports which appeared regularly in the *Journal of Commerce*. Well-thumbed copies of this paper could always be found in both the Liberal and the Constitutional Clubs; and hardly a day, certainly no week, went by without news of a ship with which some Nefyn family or other was deeply concerned. More often than not the news was routine; a ship had sailed or arrived, or been reported so many miles from her destination. Sometimes the news was more dramatic; a ship could be overdue or in serious difficulties after storm damage, so that we could only hope and pray for the best. All too often it could be tragic, as on a certain day not long after the war.

The day itself was quiet enough, but it followed a week of anxiety when the shores of southern Britain were lashed by heavy gales. Among the ships which felt the full weight of the storm was the *SS North Anglia*, which left Falmouth in ballast and immediately ran into trouble. We did not know this at the time, but later there were subdued rumours that perhaps the ballast might have been hurriedly stowed, the hatches not properly secured, and sheets of tarpaulin and other potentially dangerous gear left loose on her decks. Whatever the truth of such allegations, shortly after she left Falmouth her gear did in fact run wild, with calamitous results. As she entered the Bay of Biscay she was struck by a huge sea which nearly capsized her and started a train of disasters which had repercussions in more than one Nefyn family.

One of her officers was Captain Robert Williams 'Mona View'. When the sea struck the ship, he happened to be close to one of the hatches which was partly dislodged by the blow. He was thrown headlong into the hold, and, when he reappeared some moments later, he was first spotted by another Nefyn man on board, Peter Jones 'Tanymaes'. According to Peter Jones, he looked like a sleep-walker, his left arm hung helplessly at his side, and part of his scalp lay like a curtain over his eyes. It was with great difficulty that he could be persuaded to lie down in a comparatively sheltered spot while his scalp was sewn back into place with a curved needle. During the operation he lapsed into a coma which was to last for days.

Because of the widespread damage on board, the ship returned to Falmouth, where Robert Williams and the other casualties were taken to hospital. Three days went by before he recovered consciousness, but he never recovered the use of his left arm, and a deep hole in his temple served as a further reminder of what he had gone through. Despite his injuries, he remained on active service for another 12 years.

He was one of the lucky ones. Among the less fortunate members of the crew were four sailors from Nefyn whose injuries proved fatal. They included two of the sons of Mr and Mrs Jones 'Penpalmant'. Their coffins were brought by rail from Pwllheli, from where they were carried on a horse-drawn hearse to the new cemetery in Nefyn. Every local man and boy who could walk must have gone to Bryn

Cynan to meet them, and it was a huge, sombre procession, led by ministers and other local representative, which made its way slowly over the last mile.

When we reached 'Y Groes', we stopped for a few moments outside Penpalmant and witnessed one of those incidents which it is impossible to forget; for suddenly, at the top of the steps which climbed like a fire-escape up the front of Penpalmant, old Mrs Jones tottered into view, sagged against the railings, and bowed her head in a gesture of blank despair. It would be hard to imagine a more moving sight, and afterwards in school, when we read Kingsley's lines:

'For men must work and women must weep . . . '

it was inevitable that picture of old Mrs Jones that flashed into my mind.

Such rare moments compelled us to pause and to share vicariously in the dangers which all sailors had to face, and it was inevitable that, on some Sundays, the service in chapel should take on an added significance, and that we should sing and pray with more than usual fervour 'for those in peril on the sea'.

It was equally inevitable that, in school, when we came to read such poems as 'The Inchcape Rock' or 'The White Ship' or 'The Wreck of the Hesperus', our enjoyment could be occasionally blurred by a nagging suspicion that someone close to us might at any moment be required to cope with such dangers.

In other words, as we grew older, we naturally began to take a more sustained interest in our father's affairs, and to follow the details of their movements with a more discriminating and realistic eye.

---

[20] 'Flotsam and jetsam'.

19

Two Short Voyages

In one respect, we as a family were lucky. For the first 4 years after Father joined the *Monkbarns*, we had the pleasant surprise of seeing more of him that we would have dared to hope, as his two voyages were both comparatively short (6 months and 15 months respectively), and brought him back at not unreasonable intervals to British ports.

The first of those two voyages, from Cork to Buenos Aires and back, was noteworthy on at least two counts. For one thing, it was Father's first peace-time trip since 1914. It also demonstrated that the *Monkbarns* deserved her reputation of being 'a lovely ship'.

She left Cork in ballast on the 23rd July 1919 and took 59 days to reach Buenos Aires – nothing to crow about but nothing to be ashamed of, either. Midway through November she left Buenos Aires for the U.K. with a cargo of linseed. We all knew that she was scheduled to leave port at approximately the same time as 3 other British full-riggers – *Falkirk*, *Milverton*, and *William Mitchell* – and one 4-masted barque, *Bellands*, all similarly laden with linseed. What we did not know until we read about it later was that the 5 captains had agreed among themselves to make a race of it and to have a private wager on the result. In semi-arctic conditions the *Monkbarns* was on her best behaviour, completing the passage to Barry Roads in 47 days and winning the race by a clear margin. Her sister ship *William Mitchell* also ran true to form and came in last.

We went down to Bristol to meet Father on the last day of 1919, and after breakfast the next morning Father took me with him on the pilot's boat to Avonmouth, where the

Monkbarns waited to be towed up the river. In the Roads I had the thrill of boarding for the first time the ship which was to be Father's home for the next six years, and of being greeted on deck by her Chief Officer, Mr Stewart Wilkie, who was soon to be given command of the *William Mitchell*. Then came the further thrill of being towed up the Avon and of passing under the Clifton Bridge.

Amid all the excitement, there was one thing which bewildered me completely, for no sooner were we on board than Mr Wilkie, with a broad grin on his face, asked Father whether there was any truth in the rumour that he was about to leave the sea and to take up a job as a hospital surgeon. Everyone within earshot, including Father, seemed vastly amused, but to my 11-year-old ears such talk made no sense whatsoever, and I never plucked up enough courage to ask anyone for an explanation. It was not until more than half a century later that Captain Glasier, who was an apprentice on that 1919 voyage, told me the story behind the jest, and it is repeated here with his consent, as closely as possible in his own words:

'It was bitterly cold on that run home. Up aloft were a few men including Able Seaman X whose name for the life of me I cannot remember. As I passed below the main mast something fell on to the deck before me. It was a human finger, belonging (as I discovered later) to Able Seaman X whose left hand had been caught and mangled in a block. Two men went aloft to bring him down, and when he arrived on deck I saw that two more of his fingers were hanging loose. Funnily enough, he did not seem unduly concerned, perhaps because the intense cold had made his hands so numb that he was unaware of any pain. I took him to the Chart-house and reported to Captain Davies, who, after examining the damaged hand, ordered everybody out of the Chart-house, gave notice that he was not to be disturbed, and shut himself in with the patient. I cannot say how long the job took, but it lasted some hours. Eventually, when Able Seaman X came into the Half-deck, his left hand was swathed in bandages and resting in a sling. When asked what it felt like, he said that Captain Davies had warned him that, once the effect of the first-aid treatment had worn off, the pain would be intense, but that he must on no account disturb the bandages until we had reached port and the hand could be seen by a doctor. On the last few days of the run home, Able Seaman X suffered a great deal, but he stuck it like a Trojan, and, when at last he went into hospital in Bristol, the doctor there told him that he was a very lucky man, for, although the repairs to his hand had been done by an amateur, the amateur had done all the right things, with the result that he was likely to recover at least the partial use of all three fingers, including the one which had dropped on deck!'

During our short stay in Bristol we spent many happy hours in the Clifton Zoo, mainly in the vicinity of the bear-pit, where we used enormous ship's biscuits, tied to lengths of cord, to lure the animals up the poles. We also saw our first authentic pantomime 'Mother Goose' and responded gleefully to the novelty of such chestnuts as: 'What did the ear-wig say? . . . 'Ere we go!' . . . It all ended too abruptly when orders came for the *Monkbarns* to move on to Cardiff, where she was to remain, berthed in the East Bute Dock, until the end of July 1920.

It was shortly before leaving Bristol that we heard of Mr Wilkie's promotion to the *William Mitchell*, a prospect which his fellow-officers advised him to face with fingers crossed. His place as Mate was taken by Richard Davies of Nefyn – better known as 'Dick Isfryn' – an appointment which gave Father peculiar pleasure, since it was under the command of Dick's father that he had spent some of his earliest years at sea on the *Eivion*.

Cardiff in those days was an attractive town, and we went ashore almost every afternoon. On our way from the ship to the nearest tram terminus, we invariably stopped at the 'Golden Goat' to pass the time of day with its owner, Mr Jones – known, inevitably, as 'Jones the Goat'. A friendly and ebullient conversationalist, he was also a mine of information about the movements of men and ships, and generations of young sailors must have consulted him before signing on, as he knew precisely which vessels were well found and which should be avoided like the plague. He was also the main pillar of the local Seaman's Mission.

We would then move on to visit the shops and arcades, to savour the delights of Roath Park with its ice-cream stalls, sparkling lemonade which danced uncontrollably up one's nostrils, and boating on the lake. We also called on friends like Mr and Mrs Picton Davies, who lived with their daughter Enid in Roath Court Place, and whose hospitality knew no bounds. Mrs Davies was a native of Caernarfon, being the eldest daughter of Captain and Mrs David Jones, Gelert Street. She lost her father in 1896 when, at the early age of 53, he died and was buried at sea. Mr Picton Davies was a Carmarthenshire man, but he too had spent some 7 years in Caernarfon, as sub-editor on the staff of the *Herald*, before returning South in 1914 to join the editorial staff of the *Western Mail*. He recorded some of his experiences in a delightful book which appeared in 1962 under the title of '*Atgofion Dyn Papur Newydd*'.

For those of us with sporting interests, Cardiff had much to offer. It was a time when the Cardiff City soccer team had begun its rapid climb towards the top of the tree, when the legendary Albert Jenkins of Llanelli was the rather unpredictable star of the Welsh Rugby XV, when the equally legendary Jimmy Wilde was busy dazzling experts in the USA, and when the local press held its breath as it speculated whether there was any truth in the rumour that the heavy-weight champion of Europe, Georges Carpentier, was about to be married. So much importance was attached to these matters that they sometimes spilled over into the world of politics, as was impressed upon us whenever we passed through the covered market in the Hays. Somewhere in the background of that enormous arena there was a gramophone which churned out a constant stream of raucous popular songs, of which the favourite was a ditty which had obviously been composed before Lloyd George's popularity began to wane, because each one of its innumerable verses listed some of his achievements and then ended with a variant of the following chorus:

'When Wells fought Carpentier, then who refereed?
Lloyd George of Criccieth, look you, yes indeed!'

One sunny afternoon, while sitting on a bench near the City Hall, we were greeted by a studious-looking but cheerful young man with a bundle of books under his arm. This was Robert Davies Owen 'Erw Goch', a younger brother of the Mr Harry Owen who had urged us on to help the war effort by promising 'to kill the Kaiser Bill'. Robert Davies Owen had gone to sea as a boy during the war, saw his ship torpedoed, spent several days in an open boat in near-arctic conditions, narrowly escaped frostbite, was ordered by his doctor to abandon any notion of a life at sea, and decided to register as a student at the Cardiff Medical School. We did not know it that afternoon, but he was destined to do uncommonly well in his chosen career, to settle down in Cardiff for the rest of his life, and to establish an enviable reputation as an Ear-Nose-Throat consultant. He retired in the 1960s.

For my brother and myself, the most exciting things in

Cardiff happened on board ship. The cargo of linseed had attracted hordes of rats which could be heard scurrying behind the bulkheads of the saloon and sleeping quarters at all hours of the day and night. They infested the boats, invaded the lazaret and sail-locker, and treated the empty holds as their own special domain. To go below decks was an eerie experience, for the first impression of almost total darkness was quickly dispelled by the countless pinpoints of light incessantly on the move, the audible swishing of feet, and the friendly chirruping sound which might have come from an aviary. The rats were not unusually large but they were fast and elusive, and had defied the attempts of more than one professional rat-catcher to destroy them with dogs, traps, and poison. For some time therefore it was left to the crew, more especially the apprentices, to tackle the problem, which they did by organising rat-hunts in which (if it was known that our parents were ashore) my brother and I were allowed to join. One tactic was for a group of hunters to rustle the rats out of the boats and force them to jump on to the deck, and for a second group, armed with brooms, to hit them as they landed, so that they flew over the side into the water. It was much later that we discovered this to be a serious breach of local health regulations. My brother, despite his tender years, was outstandingly useful in these campaigns. With a broom in his hand, he had a fluent swing, and his timing was impeccable – virtues which he demonstrated later at both Cricket and Rugby.

On the 26th June 1920 the *Monkbarns*, laden with coal, set off on a round trip which lasted 15 months and included Las Palmas, Newcastle, Sydney, Iquique, and Cape Horn. Between Las Palmas and Newcastle she ran into a severe gale and mountainous seas south of Cape Town – a foretaste of what she was to suffer in 1923. The storm itself did no great damage, but, when the winds suddenly died away, she began to roll so badly that the fore and main topgallant backstays carried away and the masts went overboard, leaving her to complete the passage under topsails only.

In Iquique, during the Spring and early Summer of 1921, she languished without a freight while coming events cast their shadows over her. All too clearly, the era in which she had had such a useful part to play was rapidly drawing to a close. Quite apart from the post-war slump which affected everyone, there was also a growing conviction among men of business that sailing ships were an anachronism in the ruthlessly streamlined world of modern commerce. After the *Monkbarns* had been away for about a year, with no visible prospect of turning her bows for home, we as a family in Nefyn had resigned ourselves to the thought that she might have to go on making abortive trips to and fro across the Pacific until her bottom dropped off. We could therefore hardly believe our ears when we heard that she was on her way home with a cargo of Nitrate. Her orders were to reach the Channel and there await instructions. She berthed in Falmouth, and midway through September my mother and my brother joined her there.

When Father eventually came home on leave, his throat was marked by a scar which we children could hardly have failed to notice, but which, either from shyness or from sheer cussedness, we chose to ignore, and no member of the family ever alluded to it at that time in my hearing. Several years went by before an explanation was provided, once again by Captain Glasier:

'We were sailing in ballast from Las Palmas to Newcastle NSW, and Captain Davies had gone below to check that everything was ship-shape. As he was walking in one of the holds, along the narrow battens which served as 'floors', the ship gave a sharp, sudden lurch which threw him off balance so that he slipped and fell between two boards. At least, his body somehow or other squeezed through, but his head was trapped, with the result that he was caught dangling, with a deep gash in his throat. It took us some time to discover where he was, and, after releasing him as carefully as we could, the Mate, the Steward, and I took him to the Charthouse, where he lay back on the couch so that his wound could be dressed. It soon became obvious that it would require several stitches. It became equally obvious that the Mate, as he prepared to thread the needle, felt in no way equal to the task; and I certainly couldn't blame him, as I doubt very much whether I could have coped any better. Captain Davies quickly sized up the situation and sent John Roberts the Steward to fetch him a mirror, a glass tumbler, and a bottle of whisky. Although he was a teetotaller, he poured himself a stiff tot and slowly swallowed it. He then took the needle from the Mate, told the Steward in Welsh to hold the mirror so that he could see what he was doing, and calmly proceeded to stitch his own throat. It was all done with the utmost deliberation, and ranks in my mind as one of the most courageous actions that I have ever witnessed.'

20

Bruges and Birkenhead

From Falmouth *Monkbarns* was ordered to Bruges to discharge her cargo of Nitrate, and on the 20th September 1921 three tugs began the task of towing her across the Channel to her new berth. The operation took five days, mainly because part of the time the Channel was shrouded in thick fog and on at least one occasion *Monkbarns* came within a few feet of being rammed by a passing steamer whose skipper presumably considered that a continuous blast on the siren was somehow equivalent to a pair of eyes. My brother still remembers the shivers that ran down his young spine as the steamer's bows hove into view for a few seconds before veering away into the gloom. Having safely made Zeebrugge, they then followed the canal which runs in a straight line towards the city of Bruges until they came to a short stretch of water standing at right angles to the main canal. In that secluded corner the Germans had built some military barracks and eight concrete U-boat shelters. There *Monkbarns* was to remain for the next sixteen months, during which time our family virtually had two homes. Since Father was tied to his job and managed only rarely to take time off for the long trip to North Wales, Mother and my brother joined him on board for the duration, and on every school holiday of any length my sister and I went out to complete the family circle.

From September 1921 until January 1923, while the *Monkbarns* was based in Bruges, the entire crew numbered no more than three – Father, Dick, and 'Sails' Robinson. The first two stayed on because they were officially required to do so, but the third was there because he had no wish to be anywhere else.

A native of Dundee, 'Sails' was a grizzled widower with two daughters of whom he was extremely fond and with whom he kept up a regular and voluminous correspondence, but no amount of family affection could alter the fact that, unless he could feel the deck beneath his feet, he was like a lost soul. Consequently, it was rarely indeed that he went home to Dundee; equally rarely did he go ashore. Throughout the 18 months spent in Bruges, only once were we able to tempt him down the gangway; this was to see the lights and decorations in the town on Christmas Eve 1921, and he yielded then only because Mother was quietly insistent and he was by instinct a gentleman. We showed him everything that the bright shops and streets had to offer, but he seemed unimpressed by what he saw.

Left to himself, 'Sails' would always choose, weather permitting, to lean his elbows on the rail, puff away at his short black pipe, and stare into the distance. His normal occupation naturally took him to the sail-locker, where it was fascinating to watch him at work, with a huge expanse of canvas across his knees, pushing the big needle through with the aid of a leather 'palm'. But during the months in Bruges he had other duties as well, for he had volunteered for the official post of cook and bottlewasher. In that capacity he spent most of his time in the galley, where during the day he prepared the meals and in the evening settled down in the warmth of the stove to suck his pipe, draw upon his memories, and talk to himself. He knew that there was a standing invitation for him to join us in the saloon, but he frankly preferred his own company – not surprisingly perhaps, since he had so much to offer himself.

A keen, retentive reader of prose and verse, with Scott as his favourite author, he knew by heart enormous stretches of narrative poems like 'Marmion' and 'The Lady of the Lake' which he loved to recite to himself for hours on end. Most of the time we respected his privacy, but once in a while Dick would tempt us after supper to leave the saloon and tiptoe towards the galley, so that we could hear 'Sailor' declaiming in his rich booming voice. If we knocked at the door, he would courteously invite us in, tell us to make ourselves at home, and then, without a trace of self-consciousness or condescension, continue where he had left off.

(We were always under the impression that "Sails" Robertson was a native of Dundee. However, following a visit to the wonderful Signal Tower Museum in Arbroath, which features exhibits about "Sails" and the Monkbarns among many others, it was established that he was, in fact, from Montrose, about ten miles away from Arbroath. He was born in 1855 and died at the Dundee Royal Infirmary in 1929, at the age of 73 or 74, and was buried in Sleepyhillock Cemetery in Montrose. That, of course, means he was 70 or 71 years of age when his final voyage, presumably on the Monkbarns, ended.)

In a very short time our parents found that they were part of a small but friendly community. Alongside the *Monkbarns* was one Italian ship, and two more were astern. Of these three ships, which were under the command of Capitani Graziano, da Costa, and Mazzoni, two at least had an interesting history. Both the steel three-masted barque *Perim* (built in 1903) and the four-masted *H. Hackfeld* (built in 1890) were the product of British shipyards, having been built at the port of Glasgow for German companies (F. Laeisz and J. C. Pfluger) at a time when British workmanship enjoyed a reputation second to none. The *Perim* was registered in Hamburg, and the *H. Hackfeld* in Bremen. For years they sailed for their respective owners under the German flag, but during the war they were confiscated by the Allies, and after the War were handed over to the Italians under the general heading of Reparations.

The Italian captains were not only gregarious by nature but also eager to cement the friendship between two wartime allies. As they had recently been joined by their wives, it soon became a daily ritual for us to board each ship in turn in order to spend an hour or so sipping from small mysterious glasses and nibbling a variety of delicious biscuits. Sometimes we were surprised with something more substantial, and thus made the acquaintance of ravioli and other pasta dishes. The conversation at those sessions may not have been constructive or even coherent, but it was never dull, for even the most solemn attempts at communication were liable to explode into gales of laughter.

We also came to know some of the good citizens of Bruges itself, for in order to replenish our larder we had to pay regular visits to the shops. There were two families with whom we became especially friendly. One was that of the butcher, Meinheer Verminy Lobrecht. A hearty, well-fed man, he ran his business in the Grand'rue with the help of his equally well-fed wife and daughter. He also had a son whom we saw only at weekends because he was a student at the University of Brussels. It was he who first compelled me to speak French by asking me how many hens we had on board and insisting upon an answer. Whenever we appeared inside the shop, all other business came to a halt and we were expansively ushered into the parlour, where Father was presented with a huge cigar, the rest of us received thick slabs of plain chocolate, and all of us were expected to drink either a small glass of Vermouth or a tall beaker of Grenadine which, with occasional help from a water-jug, appeared to last forever. All the time the three of them chattered away in Flemish, the warmth of their smiles and gestures more than compensating for the fact that we could not understand a single word.

A few doors up the street was the Pâtisserie where we bought our bread, cakes, and groceries. The proprietor of this establishment was Monsieur Fasnacht, a tall, slender, gracious old man with a sparse imperial beard and gold-rimmed spectacles. Living with him were his daughter and son-in-law. They all worked hard, but he was the genius who presided over the activities in the bakery and produced the indescribable fragrance which not only filled the shop but clung to our nostrils long after we had stepped outside. The Fasnacht welcome was less boisterous than that of the Lobrechts, but it seemed no less authentic, and on cold winter days the cups of steaming chocolate which they seemed to have permanently on tap and which they insisted on our having there and then, warmed our hearts in more ways than one.

Among our more casual acquaintances ashore, two characters stand out. One was the British Consul, a tall, dark man with a bald head and toothbrush moustache, whose surname presented us with so many problems that he finally pleaded with us to call him 'Mr Joseph'. Privately, because of his striking resemblance to a well-known musician from Coedpoeth (whom we had seen in more than one 'Cymanfa') we referred to him as 'Tom Carrington' ... The other was Van Hekke, one of the station cabbies who appointed himself our personal retainer and would allow no one else to ferry us between the station and the ship. His name inspired a number of family jokes which sounded witty at the time but by now have been mercifully forgotten.

In order to reach the outskirts of the town we had to walk about a mile along a country road which ran parallel to the canal and brought us to the tram terminus, from where we clanked our way briskly to the town centre. Bruges in those days had a quiet charm which we found irresistible, and we soon came to love every feature of it – the cobblestones . . . the tall seventeenth-century houses with their wooden gables . . . the neat yellow trams with their warning bells on the roof, lurching at breakneck speed through the narrow streets before gliding smoothly into the cathedral square . . . the square itself, with its famous belfry and ranks of drowsy cab-horses waiting for a fare . . . the fruit and flower markets . . . the periodic carnivals and processions . . . the chimes from the towers and steeples . . . the novelty and infinite variety of the displays in the shop windows . . . the canals weaving their way under the hump-backed bridges . . . the dusty cinema with its French versions of such films as *Quo Vadis, The Mark of Zorro, The Sign of Four,* and *Die Niebelungen.*

Every season had its own distinctive appeal. In the Spring and Summer we could row for hours on the canal, play football on the concrete floor of the old German barracks, take a trip on one of the barges which plied along the intricate system of waterways linking Bruges with Sluis and other towns near the Dutch border, visit Ghent or Brussels, or spend a day on the battlefields of Ypres or Nieupoort.

As the war was only just over, its debris was still painfully evident. At Zeebrugge the remains of HMS Vindictive, the British destroyer which had spear-headed the famous raid by ramming the mole, still lay stranded and untouched. Further to the east, beyond Ostend, the now fashionable beaches of Blankenberg and Dixmude and Knokke were then no more than a derelict range of sand-dunes littered with tangles of barbed wire, with not a living soul in sight for miles.

Inland, of course, the desolation was even more stark and appalling. It was in a small country inn near Nieupoort, where the lunar landscape consisted exclusively of the stumps of dead trees, countless shell-holes, and the remains of sand-bagged dug-outs and trenches, that we met an English priest whom Father invited to join us for lunch, and who for the rest of the day acted as our guide. His name was Father Benedict Williamson. He told us that, during the war, he had served as Padre in the Nieupoort sector of the line, where the troops had nicknamed him 'Happy Days', and that he hoped to return once every year in memory of the friends whom he had lost. He was also the author of a book entitled 'Happy Days in France and Flanders', and the copy which he sent to my sister after returning home still survives.

As summer merged into autumn, we developed the habit of rowing in the direction of Zeebrugge, stopping at various orchards on the way to volunteer help to anyone who might need it. Since our offer was never refused, we would then spend a few hours climbing up and down ladders, carefully picking apples and pears, pausing from time to time to swallow a mouthful of home-brewed cider which made our toes curl, before calling it a day and rowing back to the ship with a bulging bag of fresh fruit in the centre of the boat, and our farmer friends on the bank smiling and waving their hands until we passed out of sight.

Perhaps the winter was the best season of all, and when the family came together for Christmas we enjoyed 3 weeks of simple but unadulterated bliss. Driving by night from the station to the ship in Van Hekke's open landau, with the horse's hooves clattering on the road and the moon shining on the canal, is one of my most nostalgic memories. Every morning as we emerged on deck, we were surrounded by enough ice and snow to satisfy the greediest appetite. The canal, between its smooth white banks, was as solid as a rock, which meant that we could safely be left to slide about at will or play improvised games with sticks and stones until Mother called us aboard for the next meal. If the weather was too cold or stormy, we spent the morning either in the galley, watching 'Sails' prepare the midday meal, or else playing in the chart-house, where Dick would drop in to give us what he called 'a lesson'. Having offered to teach my brother 'mental Arithmetic', he used to test him with such brain-twisters as: Os ydi berfa Pharo'n bedair oed, faint ydi oed trol John Tincod?' . . . In the evening we read or had sing-songs and card games, cribbage being far and away our favourite . . . As Christmas approached, we serenaded our Italian neighbours with Welsh and English carols, initiated them into the mysteries of mince pies and plum pudding, or, as part of the general celebrations, joined with them in launching enormous ship's rockets.

The wintry conditions made our visits to the town even more enchanting, for over the first mile we could slide instead of walking, the town itself looked so serene and cosy under its coat of thick, clean snow, and every shop window had something rich and strange to offer. My own favourites were the confectioners' shops, where exquisite chocolate models of the cathedral, stage-coaches, canal barges, human and animal figures of all kinds, were on display. Some were offered for sale, but they were such miracles of fine skill that it seemed blasphemous to contemplate eating them.

Impressive as everything was by the cold light of day, it became almost magical after dark, when the warm light came flooding from the shops, each window was transformed into a bright, self-contained little world, and the bells from the trams and churches combined to form a musical background to the scene.

* * *

The serenity and peace came to an end on the 22nd January 1923, when the *Monkbarns* left Bruges, bound for Birkenhead, where she spent the next few weeks being fitted and loading rock-salt for Newcastle NSW.

The family arrangements remained broadly like those which had worked so well in Bruges; viz. my brother and Mother stayed on board with Father, while my sister and I joined them whenever possible. In practice this meant half-term, an occasional weekend, and a fortnight or so at Easter. Otherwise, what a change from the tranquility of the canal to the bustle of the Mersey! Whereas Bruges had been a romantic holiday for everyone, Birkenhead was full of noise and movement and a general sense of urgency. Amid the continual clatter, things were happening all the time.

The crew soon reverted to its normal size. Recruits arrived from all points of the compass, and the total establishment came to just over 30. One unusual feature was the large proportion of apprentices, all anxious to serve on one of the few surviving wind-jammers so that they could eventually claim the right to a square-rig ticket . . . Among them was a young man of 18 from Brighton called Cyril Sibun. As I was then 14 years of age, he and I spent much time together and found that we had many interests in common. We visited Goodison Park to see Everton play Middlesbrough, and fought our way to Anfield to see Liverpool lose an exciting Cup-tie to Sheffield United by two goals to one. The winning goal was scored by a bald-headed inside-left called Gillespie, who headed in from a corner, and I can still see the smile on his face and the mud on his forehead as he wheeled around in triumph.

Of the officers, the First Mate was the one whom we knew best, for Dick was both a relative and a friend, as well as one of the most amusing companions that any group of children can ever have had . . . The Second Mate, Robert Williams, was also a Nefyn man, whose losing fight against baldness produced a distinctive hair style which it would take too long to describe but which added considerably to the gaiety of life on board, especially at meal-times, when he bowed his head and showed us his handiwork in all its glory. His fellow-officers had nicknamed him 'Bindle' because of his supposed resemblance to a character of that name created during the war years by Herbert Jenkins.

One of the former apprentices who was promoted to Third Mate was a young man called Malcolm Bruce Glasier, whose parents had been prominent among the pioneers of the Labour movement in this country. His father, Bruce Glasier, was a Glasgow architect and journalist (described in the history books as 'more of a poet than a politician') who in 1900 succeeded Keir Hardie as Chairman of the Independent Labour Party. By 1923 the father had been dead for almost two years, but the mother was still alive and more than once travelled from Manchester to visit her son. I have only a shadowy recollection of her as one of those who sometimes joined us for tea and in whose presence we were supposed to be on our best behaviour, but Mother enjoyed her company and looked forward to her visits ... The son I recall much more clearly, for one of his incidental duties was to keep an eye on my brother and myself, and, whenever we looked like shinning up the rigging or exploring the sail-locker and lazaret, he was always close at hand, like a bad conscience. For that reason, we viewed him with some suspicion, but Father liked him and reckoned that he had the makings of a first-class sailor. We began to take a more friendly interest in him when we found that his mother's brother, G. S. Conway, was a Rugby Blue and a regular choice in the England post-war XV.

Years later, Captain Glasier carved out a highly successful career with the Elder Dempster and other companies, and by the 1970s had become a patriarchal figure in Liverpool maritime circles, revered by his associates as one of the diminishing band of authentic Cape-

Horners still at large in that city. He died at West Kirby in 1979.

On the 8th March 1923 the *Monkbarns* left the Mersey and began what, according to Alan J. Villiers, was 'destined to rank as an historic voyage – her last voyage, and the last voyage of any British full-rigged ship round Cape Horn'.[21] Captain A. G. Course called it 'an epic of danger and heroism'.[22] Historic or not, it certainly proved eventful and left its mark upon us as a family.

---

[21] A. J. Villiers, op. cit. p. 108.
[22] A. G. Course, op. cit. facing p. 147.

21

A Hurricane

Affairs on land, in the meantime, were developing a momentum of their own. Some 5 years previously, while the *Monkbarns* was stationed in Cardiff, the time had come for me to try my luck at moving from the Nevin Council to the Pwllheli County School. It was a mixed experience. On the one hand, the date fixed for 'the Scholarship' approached painlessly enough, since during the months leading up to it neither my mother nor my teachers even hinted that there was anything unusual in the wind, and, when the day arrived, my friends and I travelled to Pwllheli on the roof of the bus as though we were going on holiday. We enjoyed ourselves so vigorously that Robert 'Dolwen' stopped a swinging branch in full flight and soon became the owner of a shiny black eye. On the other hand, when we reached the school and tentatively lined up for the preliminaries, our high spirits began to droop, for it quickly became evident that there was a formal drill to observe, and that, unlike us, the members of the Pwllheli squad from Ysgol Troedyrallt were thoroughly familiar with every detail of it. We did our best to copy their example as they moved with ominous confidence through an exercise for which they had been trained to the minute, but, despite our efforts, we felt like a group of young donkeys who had somehow or other strayed among the thoroughbreds on Derby Day.

This feeling of comparative inadequacy persisted for a while when, in the following September, we entered the Pwllheli County School as registered pupils for the first time and began a six-year period of living (apart from weekends and holidays) away from home. As Monday was the only day which provided an early morning bus for the 7-mile trip to Pwllheli, we were obliged to spend the time from Monday to Friday in lodgings 'in the town' – an arrangement which may have had the virtue of encouraging a certain independence of spirit in normal young boys but was liable to discourage all but the most strong-minded from doing more than the minimum quota of work. Some Nefyn parents disapproved so heartily of this arrangement that, despite the excellent tuition and the high standards regularly achieved at Pwllheli, they elected to send their children to boarding schools in places like Dolgellau, Bangor, or Towyn (Merioneth), taking the view that, if children were by force of circumstances to be deprived of full parental discipline, then at least some other effective form of unbroken supervision should be provided in its place. Towyn School was especially popular with some parents, since it was a mixed school with twin boarding houses, which meant that brothers and sisters did not have to be separated. I lost the company of Robert 'Dolwen', Hugh 'Bodwyn', and many other friends in this way, but new friends from Pwllheli and Abersoch soon helped to fill the gap, and, although my academic record in school belied the efforts of an admirable staff and the exhortations of a gifted Headmaster, my personal experience of the old lodging-house system was that it had much to commend it. With congenial friends and kind landladies, Pwllheli was not a bad place to spend the week in.

It was when I stepped off the bus in Nefyn one Friday afternoon that my sister met me with the news that the Monkbarns had run into trouble and been forced to limp back to Cape Town for repairs. Some time elapsed before we were able to piece the story together into a coherent whole. For reliable details we had to wait for Father's letters, press reports in the U.K. and South Africa, and for stories brought by individual members of the crew who filtered back to Nefyn over the next few months and years. Dick and Malcolm Glasier added their own restrained versions in due course, but it was not until we read ampler accounts compiled by Alan Villiers in *Sea Dogs of Today* and by Captain A. G. Course in his official history of the John Stewart Line that we began to realise what in fact had happened to the ship after leaving Birkenhead in March 1923.

At the best of times the traditional sailing route between this country and Australia could offer a wide range of experiences. First the North Atlantic with its variable winds, then the North-East trades, followed by the Doldrums and the Line, the South-East trades, the Southern variables beyond the Cape of Good Hope, and finally the Roaring Forties. That was the route which the *Monkbarns* naturally proposed to follow, and for the first two months after leaving port all went well.

They celebrated the crossing of the Line in traditionally boisterous fashion. Eight apprentices were dipped and shaved with grease and tar in the presence of King Neptune and his Court before being presented with copies of the following Certificate:

'Whereas you, being on the 7th day of April, 1923, admitted to Our presence, have satisfied attendant Examiners, Physicians, Chirurgeons, and Mermaids of your rights in Our Realms, we are pleased to grant you all the privileges of Our Court, for which this shall be your Warrant.
  (Signed) NEPTUNE, R. M.
  Wm. DAVIES, Master.
Ship Monkbarns.'

By the 8th May she had left the Cape well behind, and all on board were beginning to congratulate themselves on having reached the Roaring Forties without mishap when, without any warning, the weather suddenly worsened. By the following day she was being battered by heavy seas and staggering along before a strong westerly gale. At first the crew were not unduly worried, because, although the sea was dangerously high and she was taking water over both rails, the wind remained steady. In any case, most of them had survived worst storms.

But, as the wind moved to the North, the gale relentlessly built up into a hurricane. Hail and sleet added to the misery of life on deck, and she began to take on even more water, which made her all the more difficult to handle. Even when they drastically reduced sail, there was no corresponding reduction in the ferocity of the wind and sea. Only the most experienced helmsmen were allowed to go to the wheel, and they were warned not to look astern.

In such conditions it was decided to heave the ship to – a manoeuvre calling for split-second timing and no small degree of luck. There was nothing wrong with the timing beyond the fact that, at the very moment when the ship came to in the line of the wind and might have expected at least a temporary respite, the wind suddenly changed direction from North to South-South-West, and she was flung down on her side into a deep trough. The log entry[23] for that day records that 'The ship gave a fearful lurch as if falling down the side of the sea'. And, as though that were not enough, her heavy cargo shifted. The noise caused by this movement is described as 'awful', but the effect was even worse, for (in Father's words) 'she went as far on her beam ends as she could without turning turtle'. At that moment neither he nor anyone else on board expected to live another hour, let alone another day.

The log goes on: 'Ship took a heavy list to starboard, being under water to the top of the rigging doublings and well over, almost to the after hatches. Ordered the lee sheets of mizzen and fore lower tops'ls to be cut away so as to lighten the pressure, which was done, and the sails blew to ribbons, easing the ship . . . Several members of the crew slightly injured'.

The entry for the next day gives details of the main damage: 'Found the 4 boats had been struck by seas, one smashed, all damaged; galley gutted out, funnel and skylight having been washed away; lamp locker gutted, with lamps either smashed or washed away, captain's room flooded, stores destroyed . . . At 7.30 p.m. Apprentice Sibun, while aloft with A. B. Evan Davies securing the port clew of the fore upper t'gall'nts'l, fell overboard and was not seen by anyone . . . All hands working in hold night and day trying to trim cargo'.

Later, Father was to report to the press on this personal tragedy: 'It was about 7.30 and pitch dark when Apprentice Sibun, aged 19, one of the lads who had crossed the line a few days before for the first time, was sent aloft with Seaman Davies. What caused the tragedy no one can tell, but the lad fell from the yard into the sea, and in the blackness of the night nothing more was seen of him . . . Nobody could tell, not even Davies. All he knew was that he heard the boy exclaim "Oh, my God!" and that was all.'

Such an event inevitably cast an even deeper shadow over the ship, as for 3 days she remained on her beam ends, pounded by mountainous seas 'as if she were a rock lying on its side', and her men were a gloomy company as they struggled non-stop to perform the miracle of forcing her back on a partially even keel. In theory, it was an impossible task, for as soon as any part of the cargo had been trimmed, it was liable to be hurled back again by the movement of the ship. In fact, it was partly achieved, and by the 11th May she was manageable enough for Father to decide to head back North and put into Cape Town for repairs. Four days later, when the winds had abated and she entered Table Bay in calm conditions, she still had a heavy list of about 40 degrees to starboard.

In Cape Town she spent the best part of a month while much of her cargo was taken out and re-stored, and the damage aloft was repaired. With time, even the shadow of young Sibun's death was partly lifted, and by Empire Day the men had recovered sufficiently to be able to play a soccer match against a team from one of the Union Castle liners in port. But the shadow would not go away, and when a steamer came into Table Bay on its way home from Australia, it transpired that one of its junior officers was a brother of the dead apprentice. When he saw the towering spars of the *Monkbarns* he asked the pilot: 'What's that tall ship over there?', and on being told he was delighted at the prospect of giving his brother such a pleasant surprise. One can imagine how woefully different the sequel proved to be.

On 9th June the ship set out once more for Sydney, but her share of bad luck had not yet run out. June in the southern latitudes is mid-winter, and she faced a long haul across a stretch of water which, at that time of year, can be violent and destructive. It lived up to its reputation. She was struck by a succession of gales and turbulent seas which swept over her, made her roll like a tub, and inflicted fresh damage. Most of her crew were laid up at some time or another with serious injuries.

Capt. Course describes one incident: 'On the night of June 15th, when the ship was running her easting down on the wild seas of the Roaring Forties, a heavy sea crashed on board, filling the whole main deck from rail to rail and threatening to sink the ship by sheer weight of water. It caught the port watch, who were working on deck, and hurled them against fife-rails, bulwarks, and stanchions. Some had broken limbs; others, including the chief officer, were badly hurt. Knocked down and lying helpless on the deck, they were in danger of being washed overboard, but the uninjured members of the port watch, assisted by the watch below, who had hurriedly turned out, helped them to safety. The chief officer and eight seamen were laid up, leaving Captain Glasier in charge of a very depleted port watch. But in spite of being short-handed, a very creditable passage of 39 days was made, and at 10.30 a.m. on July 18th the *Monkbarns* came to anchorage in Double Bay, Sydney.'

'Very creditable' the passage may well have been, but it had also been so gruelling that the sight of land proved too much for some of the men. 'In spite of their affection for Captain Davies, half the crew "jumped" her.' It was therefore with a largely new crew of foremast hands that she moved up the coast to Newcastle to load coal for Iquique.

It must have been about this time that a friend in the Nefyn Liberal Club handed me a copy of *Sea Breezes* which contained references to the *Monkbarns*. There were photographs of the ship taken in Iquique from the deck of S.S. *Ortega*, and a comment to the effect that 'great interest was taken in the old windjammer'. There was also a photograph of Father, bearing the caption: 'Captain William Davies, who has sailed her with great skill and judgment.'

There followed several dreary months of remorseless monotony. On the 59-day passage from Newcastle to Iquique she met with more heavy gales and tumultuous seas. On her way back from Iquique with a cargo of Nitrate for Melbourne, she followed the more leisurely trade-wind route and took 103 days. This was a relatively uneventful passage, with nothing more exciting to report than a few earthquake shocks and a succession of gales. From Melbourne she moved to Newcastle to load coal yet again for Iquique. In Newcastle many members of the crew were paid off. The fo'c's'le crew left almost to a man, and were replaced by some young Finns who had recently deserted from a Finnish ship – not a promising enrolment, but acceptable on the principle that beggars can't be choosers.

Leaving Newcastle on the 2nd October 1924, she sighted the island of Juan Fernandez 44 days later, and in another 11 days arrived off Iquique. This time the cargo of Nitrate was destined for Sydney – a fourth crossing of the Pacific, made in 89 days. After discharging in Sydney, she was towed to Cockatoo Island to dry dock, to have her bottom-plating cleaned. Then on to Newcastle for more coal. This was a particularly bitter disappointment for the men, who had hoped at long last to secure a wheat charter for home. But this was not to be, and the coal was ear-marked for Callao. Not surprisingly, all the young Finns paid off, and a fresh crew of British seamen signed on. On the 4th July 1925 she left Newcastle for the last time, reaching Callao in 60 days.

It was inevitable that such a long-drawn see-saw across the other side of the world should have had its effect upon the men. For us at home it was bad enough, as month followed month in an apparently endless procession, and continually deferred hope made the heart sick; but for them, on top of the hardships which they had suffered after leaving home, the frustration must have been intolerable. From time to time, as the record shows, some of those who felt that they had had enough, simply deserted; others reacted more violently. The original second mate refused duty and came home in disgrace, while one poor devil committed suicide. The rest went on, doggedly hoping for some change in their fortunes.

That change came unexpectedly, for in Callao she

seemed to have reached a dead end. This was no new experience, as she had been similarly stranded at Iquique in 1919 during the post-war slump. In 1925 the prospects were equally bleak, for the Newcastle coal trade was declining fast, and steamers rather than sailing ships were now loading Nitrate at West Coast ports for Australia. The chances are that she could have been ordered home in ballast but for some misfortune suffered by a barque called *Queen of Scots* which had been bound for London with a cargo of guano. On her way towards Cape Horn she had been dismasted in a gale and forced to return to Valparaiso, where it was judged that the damage was so extensive that she was unlikely ever to go to sea again. The *Monkbarns* was chartered to bring home her cargo, and reached Valparaiso for loading on the 17th November 1925. Two months later, on the 20th January 1926, she weighed anchor and stood out to sea. This was, in Alan Villiers' words, 'a historic departure. She was the last of the Lime-juice full-rigged ships to set out from Valparaiso for the Horn'.[24]

---

[23] Extracts from the *Monkbarns* log appear in Villiers, op. cit. and Course, op. cit.
[24] A. J. Villiers, op. cit. p. 117.

22

Homeward Bound

In Nefyn, the news that she was at long last on the homeward lap was greeted with excitement and relief, spiced with a pinch of incredulity. It must have been even more welcome to all those on board, especially to the old faithfuls who had stayed on her since March 1923 and absorbed all the punishment which the intervening months had had to offer. Before the mast, only two of those were left.

Since it had been agreed that this was to be Father's last trip before retirement, Mother had often tried to persuade him to apply for a relief and to come home by steamer, but his unvarying answer was that the owners had been so honourable in their treatment of him that he could not possibly disappoint them by failing to bring the ship back home. What he did not tell us was that for some time he had been in poor health and that more than one doctor had urged him either to come home for treatment or to go straight into hospital. Captain Rees Thomas, the future Harbour Master of Caernarfon, was then chief officer on a steamer which happened to be in Valparaiso at that time, and it was with him and his captain and fellow-officers that Father had dinner on the eve of his departure. According to Captain Thomas, he was buoyed up by the prospect of coming home, but 'he toyed with his food'.

Within 11 days of leaving port, the log entry reads: 'Captain ill in bed' . . . . Next day: 'Captain very ill. Giving him injections every four hours' . . . It was the chief officer who made these entries. He wanted to put into Talcahuano so that Father could go to hospital, but the latter insisted that the ship was bound for London. He was equally determined after they had rounded the Horn and the chief officer pleaded with him to land at Bahia, or Port Stanley, or Monte Video, or Buenos Aires... On the 28th March, when the patient was incapable of protesting, they put into Rio de Janeiro. Father was immediately taken to hospital, where he died the next day. According to A. J. Villiers, 'only a man of the prodigious strength of a sailing-ship master mariner would have hung on as long as he did'.[25] He might have added that the constant devotion shown by his chief officer also helped to keep him alive.

The decision to make for Rio was recorded in the ship's log as early as February but was not communicated to the crew until March 16th. On board was a young Tasmanian who had joined the ship at Newcastle NSW in July 1925 and who kept a private log of the voyage from Valparaiso to London. His entry for March 16th reads: 'Picked up the trade winds in the middle watch, but the wind is very light yet. We are heading for Rio de Janeiro to put the old man ashore. He has now held out as long as he could. No master cares to put into any port for which he is not bound, and it is only because he will die that our captain has at last consented that the ship should be deflected from her course. It is only that he knows that we are not far from Rio, where he may communicate with his people, that keeps him alive. He has not eaten for nearly two months; he lives only upon his will. The mate is with him day and night, and an apprentice from each watch. They can do nothing. There is no doctor. There is no one who knows what it is that is wrong. There is no one to do anything, if we did know'.[26]

We as a family had no suspicion that events had taken such a grim turn. On the contrary, we were living in a fool's paradise and preparing ourselves mentally for the kind of 'normal' life which until then we had only dreamed about. It was a blissful prospect. The only blot on my narrow personal horizon was the fact that I was soon to sit an important examination. By now I had reached the age of 17, and, as Mother had insisted upon my remaining in school 'nes daw dy dad adra', I had somehow gravitated to the Sixth Form and was within a few short months of sitting papers for the old Higher School Certificate. It was not a prospect that I relished, and my expectations were not high.

When I landed home on the last day of the Easter Term 1926, Mother had just received a cable which read: '*Monkbarns* in Rio de Janeiro. Captain seriously ill'. Early the next morning came a second cable with the news that he was dead. This blow was softened to some extent by the fact that two of my father's oldest friends were both within striking distance of Rio and promptly stepped in to offer such practical help as they could. They were Captain Jones of 'Langdale', Pwllheli, and Captain John Roberts of Criccieth (for many years Master of the *Beeswing*). At that time they were among the many Welsh seamen trading in and out of Brazilian ports, and it was not long before they heard the news. Their response was immediate. Over the next few months, at every available opportunity, they took it upon themselves to visit Father's grave to ensure that everything was done to maintain it in good order. Captain Griffith Jones, in particular, corresponded at great length with Mother, ascertained her wishes in the minutest detail, and finally arranged to have a headstone of white Italian marble placed upon the grave. By his tireless and sensitive devotion he did more than anyone else at that stage to bridge the yawning gulf between Brazil and North Wales.

(This heartbreaking letter, written by our grandfather, Captain William Davies, from Valparaiso on 20th January 1926 to his three children, has recently come to light.

"Just a line before writing to wish you everything that is good, you will all come to London to meet us I suppose, with DV [Deo Volente – God willing] we ought to be home by the end of April fine time of the year ynte?
Note Cardiff tied with Burnley in the 3rd round for the cup. Will the football season be over by the time we get home? If not we may see some games in London.
Accept fondest love and heaps of kisses, & may God bless you.
Your loving Dad."

Sadly, the much anticipated family reunion never materialised.)

The next visitor to the spot was young Richard Roberts Griffith of Llysarborth, whose first deep-sea trip took him to Rio and who sent Mother some snapshots of the grave – a gesture which placed her in his debt for the rest of her life. His example was soon followed by Willie Hughes, a cousin from Holyhead who worked with the Canadian Pacific Line and carefully tended the grave whenever he called in Rio on a regular run between New York and Cape Town. By writing to Mother after each of his visits, he continued the slow but steady healing process which Captain Griffith Jones had begun.

(Years later, in 2003, Bethan Evans, from Denbigh, visited the grave, and the following year Sian, a friend of Bethan's, and great-granddaughter of Captain William Davies, became the first member of the family to do this.)

The author of *Ships of London River* describes Father as 'a particularly popular master. He could be strict enough when it came to a matter of maintaining discipline, but normally he was the kindliest and most easy-going of men, who took great pride in his crew, and they in turn loved him'. The same view is expressed in the obituary which the Bishop of the Falkland Islands contributed to *Sea Breezes* in July 1926. The Bishop had spent much time in Father's company during his visits to Valparaiso and had come to know him well. His article begins:

> 'Towards the end of last year there arrived in Valparaiso one of the few remaining British sailing ships, the *Monkbarns*. She is certainly a fine ship . . . Her Captain was William Davies, of Nevin, Carnarvonshire . . . He had been to sea for over 40 years and was as fine a skipper as ever trod a ship's deck' . . .

After explaining how he and Father came to meet for the first time, he touches upon a matter which is worth mentioning because it played such a vital, if unobtrusive, part in the lives of most of Father's contemporaries:

> 'Besides these opportunities of meeting him, I had Captain Davies to lunch and to spend the afternoon at my house more than once. Thus I was able . . . to estimate the character of the man. He was distinctly a religious man, and attended the Holy Communion at St Paul's on more than one occasion, accompanied by some of his officers. He did not speak much about these things except in private, but his life told its own tale . . . At last the time came for the run home . . . I held a short service on board on the Sunday afternoon before she sailed on the Tuesday. This was attended by all on board' . . . He ends: 'I have written this article . . . as a slight tribute to the memory of a man for whom I had the highest regard.
> (Signed) Norman, Bishop of the Falkland Islands'.

When the *Monkbarns* left Rio for home, her Chief Officer (Captain Richard Davies) took command, with J. M.

Williams, who had been an Able Seaman when they left Birkenhead 3 years previously, as his First Mate. It proved a dismal passage, for they had to cope with light winds and contrary gales most of the way. They ran out of food and were grateful to accept provisions from the German steamer *Raimond* of Hamburg, which answered their distress signals on the 23rd June. Previously, according to A. J. Villiers, they had been reduced to hunting rats for soup, but this statement was refuted by members of the crew. In all, the trip from Rio to London took 99 days, and it was not until the 10th July that they reached the Thames and tied up at Charlton Buoys. To quote the *Liverpool Weekly Post*: 'A steamer would perhaps take three weeks ... but it is nothing short of criminal to compare such a ship as the *Monkbarns* with a steamer'.

The London *Times* also noted her arrival:

'A month overdue, the full-rigged sailing ship *Monkbarns* – one of the last five of her kind on the British register still wandering here and there over the seven seas – came into the Thames yesterday like a picture out of the romantic past.
'It is the first time that one of the rearguard of the great British fleet of full-riggers which has now passed into oblivion has been at London since the war. As they passed up the river and it was seen that the British Ensign was flying on the staff and the house-flag of a British firm, Messrs. John Stewart and Company, was on the mainmast, every steamer in the waterway sounded a siren warning.
'The crew of the dream-ship, a perfect harmony of line and contour, reciprocated the welcome in traditional style. Lined above the figurehead of Pegasus, they sang an old shanty chorus:

'Blow, bullies, blow,
For Californ-i-o!'

'Many captains and First Officers of the great liners served their apprenticeships in the *Monkbarns*. Three and a half years have elapsed since the sailer was last at a British port, and only two members of the deck crew of 24 she carried when she left Liverpool then have returned on board ...
'Since her departure from Liverpool the beautiful ship has been buffeted in 60 storms ... [She] has been 99 days on the voyage from Rio de Janeiro to the Thames, having had to encounter 33 days of head-winds, and, off the Irish coast, 15 days of unfavourable winds and calms.'

That press report proved to be her epitaph. In one small detail the *Times* was mistaken: by 1926 she was one of only 3 (not 5) square-riggers flying the Red Ensign, and this stark figure was not the only indication that her days were numbered. Her last voyage of 3 years 4 months had proved such a drain on her owners' resources that she could be described as an expensive luxury which, in commercial terms, made no sense. In the words of Mr J. A. Young, manager and sole partner of the John Stewart line at that time: 'It was a long passage and a losing one. I could no longer keep her on'.[27] For the modest sum of £2,500 she was sold to Messrs. Brun & Von Lippe of Tonsberg, Norway, for use in their whaling company the Ballenera Española; and on the 5th March 1927 she turned her back on a British port for the last time when she left Port Talbot, loaded, in tow, for Corcubion in northern Spain, to eke out the rest of her days as a coal hulk.

The *William Mitchell* and the *Garthpool* fared no better. The former left Callao on the 27th July 1927, bound, via

Tocopilla and the Panama Canal, for Ostend; and there, for the sum of £2,100, she was sold to a firm of foreign ship-breakers and ended her days on a scrap-heap.

This left *Garthpool* as the only British deep-sea sailer; and, as she sailed home from Wallaroo in the Spring of 1928, there were rumours that the Company of Master Mariners had plans to take her over with a view to adapting her as a Training Ship for Merchant Navy entrants. All such speculation ended in November 1929 when this last survivor of a glorious era struck a reef near Bonavista, one of the Cape Verde Islands, and became a total loss.

Among those who watched the *Monkbarns* move up the Thames on the 10th July 1926 was Mr M. W. Horlock of Caernarfon, then a young man working on a wharf in Charlton. A few weeks later, when the ship's crew had been paid off and her cargo discharged, he went on board, and among the litter which strewed the deck he came across a sailmaker's leather 'palm', which he salvaged and kept as a souvenir for nearly 50 years. It was not until December 1975 that he discovered my connection with the *Monkbarns*. He was then generous enough to give me the 'palm', which will be treasured as another link with a ship which played such a momentous part in the life of my family.

* * *

In 2002 we became aware of a painting entitled "In London's River" by the renowned maritime artist and historian, the Australian Robert Carter, depicting the final voyage of the *Monkbarns* up the River Thames.

We were intrigued to find out how he, an Australian from Sydney, had come to paint this scene, and which source materials he had used, and sent him an email. He was kind enough to reply, stating, "I have been researching sailing ships for most of my life. About 20 years ago I met up with a Dudley Turner, a seaman in that last voyage. He lived in Sydney. We became good friends and he told me much about that voyage as well as lending me his diary. He described that scene and it is included in a book I have written about the last sailing ships. The painting is hanging in the Maritime Museum in Hobart, bought and donated to the museum by Dudley's nephew." He also sent a copy of part of Dudley Turner's handwritten diary, and the evocative and poetic ending is quoted below:

"But what will happen to our old ship now that she is safely home, will she ever go crashing through the 'Roaring Forties' again, or know the splendour of those tropical nights, when the breeze sighs softly through the rigging? I wonder.

Oh I think my song is rather long,
Roll the cotton down,
Oh just one more pull & then belay,
Oh. Roll the cotton down."

We would like to express our gratitude to Robert Carter in allowing us to quote from his correspondence and also from Dudley Turner's diary, as well as granting us permission to reproduce his atmospheric painting. You can read more about him on his website https://robertcarter.com.au/

* * *

And what exactly became of the old "Monkbarns" after this? The author had some idea, but fortunately for us, Jay Sivell has carried out some detailed research about her grandfather, Bert Sivell, who started as an apprentice on the "Monkbarns" in 1911, becoming a captain in later life. Her research can be found online as *"Tales my grandfather would have told me. A sailor's life 1910-1941."* She also has a very informative article in the August 2014 edition of "The Cape Horner" magazine which states:

> 'It was July 1926, and Monkbarns was the first full-rigged ship to come into the Port of London for eight years, "a wandering and lonely ghost which we may not see again," wrote The Star. The Times called her "a picture out of the romantic past".
> Chips the ship's carpenter was more prosaic. "I've had six meals since I came ashore 16 hours ago," he told the Westminster Gazette, "and I'm still hungry." Monkbarns was to find only one more cargo – Welsh coal, which she delivered under tow, to her new Norwegian owners off Corcubion in northern Spain the following March. She finished her life as a coal hulk to the whaling industry – the last British full-rigged ship to sail round Cape Horn, according to Alan Villiers (Sea-dogs of To-day, 1932), still bunkering passing steamers as late as 1954.

My last sighting is from a personal letter. Brian Watson, later senior pilot/deputy harbour master at Montrose, was then a nosy British steamship apprentice in the Baron Elibank. In 1954 he spotted a name in raised letters on the nearby bunkering hulk after his ship had sought refuge in Corcubion bay during bad weather. He recognised she was an old Britisher and climbed aboard for a look round.

In 1999 he wrote: "We berthed alongside a coal hulk and I could clearly see her name *Monkbarns* the metal letters still visible on her counter stern." He said the masts had been cut down to stumps and he thought the bowsprit had been cut away, most of the deck and poop cabins had been stripped, a rusting galley stove had been moved into the poop accommodation.

Unfortunately, he was spotted by the steamer's Mate and chased back to work before he could check the bows for the little white horse. Sadly, I can find no further trace of what became of *Monkbarns*.'

However, in an email dated 6th February 2019, generously granting permission to quote from her research, she writes:

'... it now seems likely that the old ship was broken up on the wharf at Corcubion itself – possibly as late as the late 1960s.'

---

[25] ibid., p. 118.
[26] Quoted in 'The Log Book, by the Skipper', *Liverpool Weekly Post* shortly after the *Monkbarns* returned home in 1926.
[27] Quoted in A. J. Villiers, op. cit., p. 83.

IN LONDON'S RIVER: the Monkbarns by Robert Carter

23

A Tradition Ends

One of the side-effects of Father's death, and more especially of the circumstances in which he died, was that Mother, once her grief had subsided, firmly announced that my brother and I could abandon any plans which we might have had for going to sea. Although I had vaguely, almost intuitively, thought of myself as a future sailor, like all the other men in Father's family, I cannot pretend that this emphatic ban caused me any distress, perhaps because the far greater distress of losing Father had numbed my feelings, perhaps for some other reason which lay too deep for me to fathom. In any event, the way in which the facts of life had developed since the end of the War, and were to keep on developing for the next decade, might have made Mother's ban unnecessary.

The crippling trade recession from which the world had suffered for so many years meant, among other things, that sea-faring was no longer the exciting prospect which it had appeared to be to earlier generations. Sailing ships had already been written off as hopelessly out of date, and were rapidly disappearing from the scene as one famous ship after another was either broken up or sold to foreign companies to serve as whaling hulks, barges, oil tanks, wool depots, or 'country wallahs' in odd corners of the globe. Not even a tough survivor like the *Monkbarns* had long to go. Steamers also were hit hard as they came to feel the full blast of the economic blizzard.

Many Nefyn men recognised the signals and retired before their time; others who were too young for retirement but could see no future afloat tried their hand at a variety of shore jobs for which they had no formal qualifications but to which they brought the invaluable assets of resourcefulness and self-discipline. Typical of this latter group was Captain Ellis Hugh Williams, who became a School Attendance Officer in the Penygroes area before being promoted Superintendent for the County.

In such a climate, families where for generations the male members had become seamen as a matter of course, almost as though they were carried along on an invisible conveyor belt, were gradually forced to think afresh as the belt began to slow down, and a long, rich tradition ground ominously to a halt.

It is small wonder that most of the boys of my generation were persuaded not to follow in their fathers' footsteps but to seek a career elsewhere. The few exceptions in my circle of friends and cousins could be counted on the fingers of one hand.

Hugh Griffith 'Bodwyn' was a strong athletic boy who passionately loved the sea and everything connected with it. Although he went into steam, he had a deep feeling for sail, and I well remember how thrilled he was to be able to tell me that he had seen the *Gwydyr Castle* in Port Louis, Mauritius. It came as a stunning shock to his family and friends when he contracted TB and died after a short illness in his early twenties.

Wil Hughes 'Tan-y-Fron', who always seemed in some strange way to be a shade more equable and mature than most of us, was drowned at about the same age when a Runciman yacht on which he was serving capsized in a gale in the North Sea, and his body was washed ashore near Scarborough.

Two cousins who similarly defied augury and doggedly followed the old traditions were lost in the Second World War. Hugh Williams 'Gwynfryn' had been Master for some years when he found himself on the notorious Northern passage to Murmansk in the depth of the Arctic winter. Like most other convoys in those grim regions, the one in which he travelled met atrocious weather conditions and intense enemy activity and, of the many casualties, Hugh's ship was one. Survivors reported that, before it finally disappeared, he was last seen standing on the bridge.

Thomas David Davies 'Isfryn' had gained his Second Mate's certificate and was delighted to be in the happy position of having to choose between two jobs – both in tankers – one in Aden and the other in Aruba. In discussing his choice, he expressed the view that, if he went to such an exposed area as the Red Sea, he would be a sitting target for Axis raiders, and that it clearly made better sense to cross the Atlantic to the relative safety of the Dutch West Indies. Hardly had he arrived there than a German U-boat penetrated the harbour defences one night, launched a series of torpedoes, and transformed the harbour into an inferno. Not a single tanker escaped, and hundreds of sailors (including poor Thomas) were either killed outright by blast or else burned to death.

Thomas's closest friend was Henry Parry of Muriau, Stryd y Plas. With a father and several uncles who were Master Mariners, it was almost inevitable that Harry should also try his hand at sea-faring, but indifferent health soon put an end to the experiment and he became a dentist instead. After graduating at the University of Liverpool, he spent some thirty years preserving the teeth of generations of children in the schools of Lleyn. His links with the sea, however, remained unaffected by the change, and his interest flowed into new channels. The local branch of the National Lifeboat Institute was only one of numerous organisations which benefited from his support; over the years he produced a sequence of books and pamphlets and articles on various aspects of local maritime history; perhaps most important of all, he also decided to collect all the maritime documents and photographs relating to the area that he could lay his hands upon. I can clearly recall the astonishment and even disbelief with which his other friends and I received the news that he was embarked upon such an extraordinary project. To us, who had far more immediate interests to occupy our time, it seemed rather a pointless exercise, like cornering pound-notes in a market that was well and truly flooded with them. We were cute enough to be supercilious but not bright enough to realise that time was on Harry's side. By today the unique collection which he so painstakingly compiled is a highly prized possession of the Gwynedd Archives Service and likely to be a happy hunting ground for many a future historian and researcher.

One old friend and neighbour survived everything that circumstances had in store for him. Richard Roberts 'Llysarborth', who did his pre-service training on *HMS Conway*, eventually became a tanker captain with the Shell company and saw service throughout the Second World War and beyond before retiring to live with his wife and son in Edern, where, until his sudden death in the Spring of this year, he enjoyed a well-earned respite from the cares of yesterday.

As for the rest of us, we broke completely with the past and set our faces towards new ways of life which had never figured in our fathers' plans. But that is another story...

Epilogue

Of the many privileges which we enjoyed as children, perhaps the greatest was that of being allowed to rub shoulders with some of the last representatives of that unique breed of men who insisted on going down to the sea in sailing ships, despite the rival attractions of modern science. If a fitting epitaph were needed for such men, it can be found in an article by Captain M. B. Glasier which appears in Volume XI of *Sea Breezes* and was written by him in 1927 after he had visited one of his former shipmates, Captain Stewart Wilkie, aboard the *William Mitchell*:

> '. . . There were many men in those days to whom the comparative ease and security of steam were possible, but who quietly remained in sail, undergoing hardship and peril and personal discomfort, voyage after voyage, year after year, and never dreaming of giving it up . . . Condemn them for lack of ambition, prejudice, refusal to move with the times, anything you wish, but to me the explanation is different. These men, sailing their tall ships through the waters of the seven seas, encountering, combating, and overcoming all the wilful idiosyncrasies of Mother Ocean when she opposed them, working with her and by her when, in benign mood, she favoured them with fair conditions, these men practised a craft – sea-craft. They wrought from the four winds the propelling power of their vessels, dealing with Nature always, making her serve their ends, take them whither they wished to go. And I maintain that no man may be blamed

for giving his life to a calling at once so honourable, so exacting, and so in harmony with the eternal scheme of things. A calling imbued with romance and beauty unknown to the ordered security of steam . . . '

With hindsight it is easy to realise how lucky we were to live through the closing years of such a bright, heroic period in Welsh maritime history, and it seems a pity that we did not realise it at the time. A pity, but hardly surprising, for only exceptional boys are born with an active sense of history, and we were not exceptional boys.

A review by Iorwerth Roberts of the first edition of *Growing Up Among Sailors*, *Daily Post*, 1983

Salty yarns

When the good ship *Monkbarns* sailed out of Valparaiso on January 20, 1926, she was the "last of the Lime-juice full-rigged ships to set out from Valparaiso for the Horn."

Her captain that day was a man of Nefyn, William Davies, a veteran of 45 years of sail, making what he intended to be his last trip before his retirement.

But he was never destined to sail her home, for he was taken so seriously ill that his mate took her in to Rio de Janeiro, where her master died on March, 29.

She was one of the last three of her kind and this her last voyage brought her to the Thames a month overdue, to a welcome of sirens. During that last trip of three years and four months, she had been a buffeted by 60 storms and even on the 99 days from Rio she had encountered 33 days of head-wind.

Williams Davies' son, John Ifor Davies, in a remarkable book about his childhood "Growing Up Among Sailors" published by the Gwynedd Archives Service (£3.95), brings to life the courage of the men who went down to the sea in ships and equally of their women-folk.

As a bride, his school-teacher mother, accompanied her husband on the first of several vayages and until schooling intervened he and his older sister travelled the world on a sailing ship.

He was only a few weeks old when he set off on the first voyage to Melbourne and was not quite four when he hung up his childhood sea-boots.

They were not luxury cruises, as one hair-raising story about a captain's wife trapped in the stateroom holding her child above her head as the water reached her armpits, illustrates.

His is a record of the hardship of seafaring, laced with memories of a childhood spent among seaferers in a coastal town famous for its mariners. Mr Davies, former headmaster of Ysgol Sir Hugh Owen, Caernarfon, has written a worthy requiem to his father and to the age of sail.

Other Maritime books from Gwasg Carreg Gwalch

www.carreg-gwalch.cymru

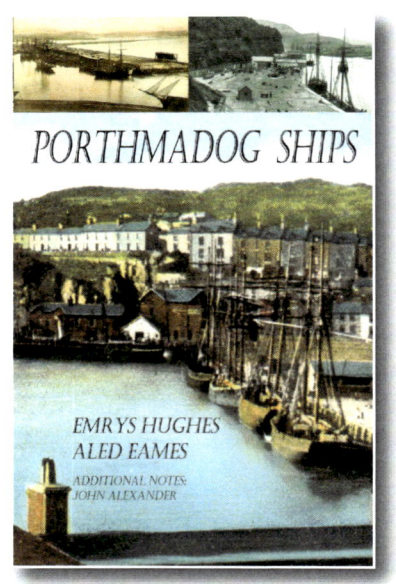

PORTHMADOG SHIPS

Emrys Hughes
Aled Eames

£18

The late Emrys, grandson of one of the most successful master mariners of Porthmadog, had over many years collected much information about the vessels, which he and his family knew well.

In order that Emrys Hughes's gazetteer of Porthmadog ships (compiled in the 1930s-40s, when there were still many survivors of the age of sail around Porthmadog) should be made available to a wider public, the Gwynedd Archives Service invited Aled Eames, the eminent maritime historian, to edit Emrys Hughes's manuscript, and add chapters on Porthmadog as a maritime community, on the ships and their builders and the seamen.

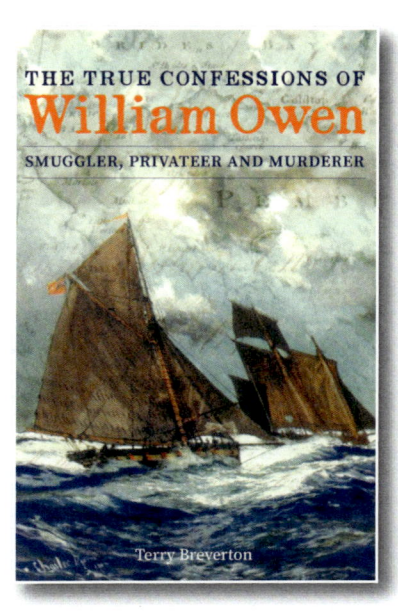

The True Confessions of WILLIAM OWEN Smuggler, Privateer and Murderer

Terry Breverton

£8.50

A strange man, who thought nothing of killing unarmed men in cold blood ... the book examines the truth and lies of his remarkable life.

SHIPS AND SEAMEN OF ANGLESEY 1558–1918

Aled Eames

£18

The book is illustrated with drawings, maps and photographs and is essential for the understanding of the significance of the maritime history of Wales.

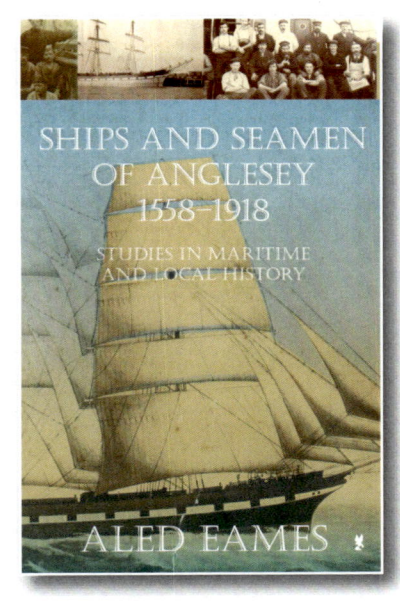

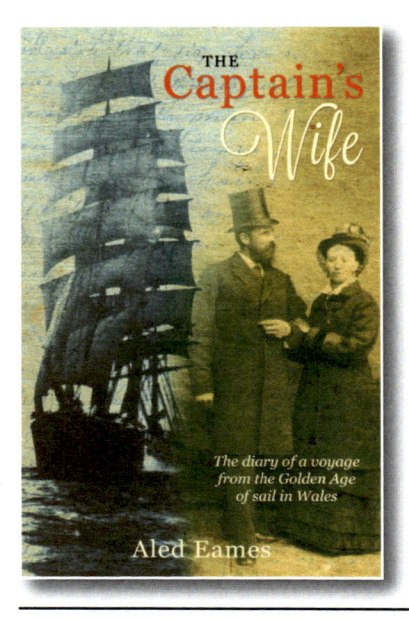

THE CAPTAIN'S WIFE

Aled Eames

£8.50

It is a tribute to a generation of women who faced great dangers at sea but also travelled the world with their master mariner husbands.

BORTH: A MARITIME HISTORY

Terry Davies

£8.50

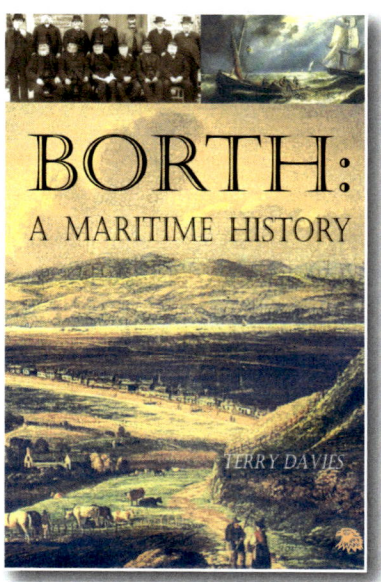

Borth, a small seaside village in Ceredigion, is mainly known nowadays as a holiday location, but formerly it was full of seafaring families – Merchant Navy, Royal Navy, fishermen and lifeboatmen. Terry Davies, a Borth man himself, tells here of the voyages, the tragedies and the triumphs, of the intertwining branches of the family trees.